TAROT: TEMPLE OF PAPER, HOUSE OF CARDS

TAROT: TEMPLE OF PAPER, HOUSE OF CARDS

Understand the Tarot from medieval
roots to modern readings, its archeology
of self and its architecture of heaven

CARLOS ESCOBEL

gatekeeper press

Columbus, Ohio

Tarot: Temple of Paper, House of Cards: Understand the Tarot from medieval roots to modern readings, its archeology of self and its architecture of heaven

Published by Gatekeeper Press
2167 Stringtown Rd, Suite 109
Columbus, OH 43123-2989
www.GatekeeperPress.com

The cover design, and editorial work for this book are entirely the product of the author. Gatekeeper Press did not participate in and is not responsible for any aspect of these elements.

eISBN: 9781642377293
ISBN (paperback): 9781642378436

"We've all been taught in looking at pictures to look for too much. Something in the child's delight in playing with colors and shapes has to be restored to us before we learn to see again, before we unlearn the terms in which we ordinarily see."
—The Language of Vision

CONTENTS

INTRODUCTION

Fig 1 - Photo by Gertrude Bell (1911).

"I like ruins because what remains is not the total design, but the clarity of thought, the naked structure, the spirit of the thing."[1] Acclaimed architect Tadao Ando

ALL WE HAVE left of the Tarot is a set of ruins, the cards themselves. They are as mysterious to most as an archaeological find from a lost civilization. Was this building a house of worship or a palace? What do certain symbols on it mean? With work we can get closer to the truth but never fully realize it.

There is something innate about degraded, mysterious stone remnants that calls out to us. Despite our ignorance about them we understand that they are important, that their design speaks to an ancient wisdom, that the builders understood something we don't even though there is much we understand that they didn't.

Tarot cards have that same quality for many. And we don't know too much more about them than we do about our hypothetical ruins. There is some documented history and many context clues to be sure but we don't have the totality, in fact far from it. The Tarot has been the subject of author explorations (and inventions) for over 200 years and has existed for over 500. The writings therefore lagged behind the objects and their use considerably.

Since no real explanations were left with the ruins, all of the writers could only, in large part, speculate (and I'm no exception). However what eventually started as speculation evolved into unintended dogma in many cases. You will often hear someone learning about the Tarot talk about rules and concepts as if they were brought down from the proverbial mountaintop. You shouldn't read for yourself, you can't buy your own deck, you have to *cleanse* your cards before you use them, if a card comes out reversed it has a different meaning, the cards are an expression of hermetic philosophy, are used with astrology, etc. There is nothing inherently wrong with most of those thoughts or the countless other bits of lore. It is just important to know it was all invented long after the cards were and it is not mandatory to believe in or practice any of it.

What should be mandatory is to understand the heart of the art, the naked structure, the spirit of the thing. Users should know how the cards are both never and ever changing and how almost impossibly complex and multilayered they are. This book attempts to help with that by writing about them and their use in a completely new way. Because of that I hope it turns out to be highly useful for beginners and experts alike. Part of that new way involves bringing up new things. The only bold claim I will make is the following; the thesis of this book is entirely new as are many of the facts presented herein.

*   *   *

When trying to explain a complex concept to someone, we instinctively reach for a metaphor. This is the most efficient way to get them to grasp the essence of what is an alien and confusing subject from their perspective.

But what metaphor, analogy, etc. fits this amorphous thing that has significantly changed over the centuries, and is still changing today? The book's title hints at the answer. It's also hinted at in the following quotation about a different subject.

"Visual analogy is a cognitive tool for problem solving and clarification of complex conceptual or linguistic thought." *Acting On the Path to Awakening: A Cognitive Exploration of Identity Transformation and Performance in Vajrayana Deity-Yoga*[2].

Ancient, partially understood artifacts are fascinating on a number of levels from the artistic and historic to the religious and philosophical. The same is true of this one. In addition to my overall thesis, you'll therefore find a robust defense of the Tarot in the pages that follow but not of it as a divination tool in the classic sense (e.g. fortune telling). It is an object and practice well worthy of study, use and appreciation regardless of whether or not it can do what some claim.

And fear not when it comes to what it can do as far as this book is concerned. I may not believe the cards can tell the future or read distant minds . . . from my experience the most commonly posed questions boil down to those two categories. But what I believe they can do is most impressive. Whether you feel clairvoyant abilities exist or you are a complete rationalist, I hope you'll end up agreeing that a peculiar thing about the Tarot is that it can work regardless of what anyone believes. But to appreciate why that is, what they are and what they do, let's proceed.

CHAPTER 1
THE ACCIDENTAL ORACLE

"The word Tarot is not yet a household word in England, it is necessary to premise that the Tarot is a pack of playing cards, seventy-eight in number, which pack has been in some limited use as a game of cards in parts of Italy, Germany, and France for several centuries. Like the pack of fifty-two cards, its origin is enveloped in mystery . . . the Tarot cards form a concentrated essence of the mysterious knowledge of the ancient world . . . Yes, the game of cards called the Tarot, which the gypsies possess, is the Bible of Bibles. It is the book of Thoth, Hermes Trismegistus, the book of Adam, the primitive revelation of ancient civilizations." *Ars Quatuor Coronatorum* (Freemasons Lodge No. 2076, London) 1892, partially quoting from *The Tarot of the Bohemians* by M. Papus.[3]

THE ARCHDUKE OF AUSTRIA CONSULTING A FORTUNE-TELLER.

Fig 2 - Much art concerning the Tarot throughout history
involved the upper crust of society looking for guidance
as in this example.

OUR OPENING QUOTATION admirably condenses the
Tarot's origin, structure and evolution as it has existed
in the popular consciousness, gross misunderstandings
and all. It is no simple thing to try and explain the Tarot as those
confusing words from long ago attest. How can something be a
European society game, a gypsy artifact and the sum teachings
of the great pre-Christian civilizations? Well it can't actually but
as things turn out that doesn't mean it is any less fascinating,
profound or simply useful of a thing.

It was in fact as stated by our Freemason author, originally
a European card game whose roots and invention are mostly a
mystery tied to the overall advent of playing cards in Europe.
That advent took place in the 14th century as the practice was
imported from the Islamic world, likely through Egypt and the
Mamluk cards as they are known.[4] This was the result of a long

transmission of the use of cards from the Far East. China is generally considered the birthplace of playing cards with their invention happening as late as the 12th century.[5] Of all the card games that eventually evolved in Europe, the Tarot in particular was imbued with mystical teachings in later centuries. This started early, in writing as far back as the late 18th century. The shift was however progressive and really took hold around the time of our late 19th century Freemason writing.

The Tarot has been called an optical language, a nomadic cathedral, "the Devil's picture books" and more.[6] Even people who regularly read the cards can find it difficult to describe and no two descriptions seem alike. Why the difficulty? Let's understand its origin and evolution a bit more to answer that question.

It didn't take long after the adoption of playing cards in the West for the Tarot to be invented in northern Italy, somewhere around the early 15th century. That estimate though is a guess based on the earliest known written mentions of it. We can reasonably speculate it had already been in existence for some time prior to the earliest surviving notations about it but who is to say?

We don't know which northern Italian city saw the Tarot's birth but it is certain that the game quickly spread to others. Often a municipality would slightly alter the deck, creating their own particular spin. The evolution of the cards was therefore present from the very start.

Regardless, at first it was a privilege of the aristocracy. This is why the oldest surviving examples are sumptuously decorated works commissioned by wealthy patrons. It eventually spread to the masses though, especially after mass production printing techniques became increasingly common. There is some indication that predictive and/or personality reading became a part of the game early on but as more of a harmless parlor game.[7] This was long before it was ascribed overtly mystical properties by later writers and users.

The creation of the Tarot did not then occur in a vacuum, it was part of Europe's adoption of a foreign object and its use, the aforementioned playing cards. They are also just part of a larger tradition called *cartomancy*, divining through the use of cards. Many old paintings show gypsies telling fortunes with cards that are clearly from non-Tarot playing decks.

There is even the real possibility that what we would consider non-Tarot cards were the first ones used for divination. For instance a mid-15th century card game in Spain called *Juego de Naypes* or Game of Cards had verses written on the cards that were used to divine romantic matters about the players.[8]

The Tarot was a landmark change in any event and just as its beginnings had connections to other cards, so did its future in that the original game played with them is the precursor to the game of bridge.

The similarities and differences between a modern pack of bridge or poker cards and a Tarot deck will be readily apparent to anyone who compares them. The 22 *major arcana* cards are the heart of that difference and they seemingly have little connection to the other, more systematic and typical playing cards of the Tarot deck. These *atouts* acted as trump cards in the game (so we will also call them *trumps*). It is possible but not probable that they were an entirely separate creation that was simply added to a standard deck of cards at some point. Much scholarship has been done by diligent researchers in an effort to determine exactly how the game of Tarot came to be with no definitive answers yet found.

Regardless of how it all came to be, it was the major arcana that made this kind of card deck particularly but not exclusively prone to metaphysical interpretation and use. The exact origins and intentionality behind those 22 cards are mostly lost to time.

They may even have been born out of an earlier, completely different set of atouts based on Greek mythology. We are though, fortunately, not here to try and solve the mystery of the Tarot's birth.

* * *

Most of the pedagogy around Tarot as anything other than a straightforward card game was created in the 19th and 20th centuries, practically half a millennia after the first cards were made and used. To make things more confusing, the original written esoteric interpretations of our mysterious ruins were pure conjecture and postdated the cards themselves by about 350 years. They were also the beginning of a never-ending trend.

All of this is why it can be so many different things to so many different people. To some it is a simple game, one still played in parts of Europe. For others it is a penetrating psychological exercise; a manifestation of Carl Jung's archetypes and theory of the collective unconscious. Meanwhile many today consider it an expression of modern occultist beliefs (e.g. various mystical traditions).

I was writing a book on the Tarot where I deal with all of this, or at least try to, when a tangential thought came to me. It was a thought I couldn't shake, actually a question. As mentioned in the Introduction, that question is: What is a good metaphor for the Tarot? What especially is one that can help us understand what it is instead of what different parties think it should be?

Here is a warm up exercise of sorts . . . Imagine if chess had transitioned from the game you know today into a ritual that was personal discovery for some, divination for others. The 32 pieces on 64 spaces can form millions of unique combinations. That's why seemingly no two games play out exactly the same. So, what if people started using pieces like the white king, black queen, white rook, etc. as representations for different facets of humanity, divinity and the forces we are beset by in life? There would be major and minor pieces. The minor (pawns) would support the major. Playing a game or making some moves would be like the drawing the cards. An unpredictable combination of elements would result each time yet recognizable patterns would repeat as well. Dueling kings with one pawn each being all that's left on the board would for instance be something you encounter more than once. The meanings assigned to the pieces, patterns, numbers of pieces and placement on the board thereby turned a game into a tool for divination or self-exploration, depending on your beliefs. This unintended use of the chess board then went on in some quarters for centuries without being too widely known (think of gypsies providing this service along with palm reading, crystal ball gazing, etc.).

Then, in modernity this was all rediscovered and really put on the map by enthusiasts who picked up on the earlier esoteric theorizing about chess and expanded upon it. This largely involved the continued imposition of external belief systems to the ritual. Concepts from Gnosticism, Orphism, Egyptian religion, Kabbalah, Hermeticism, alchemy, astrology, numerology and more were applied to chess by various parties in various ways. Many claimed or strongly implied that these belief systems were an explicit part of chess' original intent. This was part of a much greater trend wherein the modern Western esoteric tradition appropriated countless foreign, ancient and exotic elements into their amalgam belief system at will.

And just to make things more convoluted, their conjecture had some possible but unprovable historical associations.

And just to make things more convoluted, that conjecture had some possible but unprovable historical associations. That is because symbols that could reasonably be interpreted as coming from Hermetic philosophy, etc. could be seen in the ancient chess boards. Additionally, concepts from various esoteric philosophies do feel quite appropriate as ways of understanding the chess ritual. In any case, a litany of new rules and teachings on how to use chess for divinatory purposes was created, forming practically all of the guidance that exists today.

That last bit accounts for the modern era divination revolution that Tarot cards underwent in the late 19th/early 20th century in the hands of modern occultists like the Hermetic Order of the Golden Dawn. That group boasted members like A.E. Waite, Aleister Crowley and William Butler Yeats.

Strange as it may sound, that is all a fantastic metaphor for the what the Tarot is, how it is used, how that use evolved over time and how a body of teachings and interpretations were created centuries after the cards themselves came along. In fact if you want to add geographic detail to it all, imagine chess having been invented in Italy. The later mystical use begins in France centuries later and continues to evolve there while it remains just the original game in other European countries. Eventually the secondary use catches on not just with the rest of Europe but with the world in general via a transmission to England. That is exactly how the mystical use of Tarot went global.[9]

Back to chess, think about how pawns are generic when compared to the more powerful pieces on the board. Then imagine a creative team in the modern age individualizing each pawn and people assigning corresponding meanings to them based on the now distinct images. This broke significantly with the more ancient design but it made reading easier for beginners to learn. To let my personal opinion break in for a moment, I am not saying that was an entirely good thing. Still, it greatly expanded the user base with people finding specificity and specific instructions easier to grasp. The embrace of esoteric chess therefore exploded in popularity.

That last paragraph was our chess analogy extension for the famed Rider-Waite-Smith Tarot deck which was published in 1910. It and its variants are by far the most highly used today, largely replacing traditional decks like the Tarot de Marseille (as in Marseille, France). We should note that they likely modeled their concept on the oldest known full Tarot set in existence, the gorgeous Sola-Busca deck, made c. 1470 CE. It has individual characters and scenes on all of the *minor arcana* (the other 56 cards of the Tarot). This is something that would remain an outlier though and not be embraced at large until the 20th century.

In history one revolution often begets another though so yet more change came along. Artists began redesigning the cards in an infinite variety. The seal was broken and modern variations of the images became on ongoing process. After all, why should some teams (like the Rider publishing company, creator A. E. Waite and artist Pamela Smith) be the only ones that got to redesign the cards? But practically all of these later decks are offshoots of the Rider-Waite-Smith template. These then are the equivalent of the Star Wars, Lord of the Rings, U.S. Civil War, etc. chess boards that exist today. Artists nowadays constantly reinvent Tarot card visuals in whatever way they like. I saw a Sherlock Holmes themed deck just the other day in a bookstore.

So, the alternate universe imagined above, where the game of chess became an oracle instead of the cards is a useful way to (fairly) quickly take a crash course in the history of the Tarot.

OK, we're actually done talking about chess. As much as I like that mechanism and as useful as it is for explaining the Tarot's evolution; we need something much greater to explain the

Tarot in full. The reason for this is that the deck and its use, its internal interdependencies, etc. are so difficult to encapsulate. It has a multitude of interlocking elements and overlapping aspects. That complexity may make it overwhelming at first for many and difficult to master but also gives it a depth that has allowed it to be plumbed for meaning for centuries. That is also why an individual can throw the cards for a lifetime and never tire of it, and never fail to find new lessons for themselves or others. This oracle may be accidental but it is no less profound because of it.

CHAPTER 2

THE DECK, THE CARDS AND ASSORTED FUNDAMENTALS

"... we have enough before us to enable us to adopt the Tarot cards as the earliest form of playing cards, and to see in them a distinctly Eastern symbolism. It being conceded that cards are of Eastern origin ... swept westward through Persia and Arabia, through Egypt, and along the Mediterranean into ... Europe. It is in Spain that we may reasonably look for their first foothold, and this idea is strengthened by the fact that all the earliest games of cards are of Spanish invention." *Journal of the Society of the Arts*, 1889[10]

WE DON'T KNOW if Spain was actually the first place playing cards were adopted by Europeans. There is also far less certainty than our 1889 author allows about stating that Tarot was the first card game of European origin. In fact the opposite is almost a certainty. Regardless, our takeaway is the east to west cross-cultural process described above giving birth to European playing cards. The first set made in Europe were surely copies of what they saw from abroad.

This book is not about explaining things in a user manual manner. It is also not meant to initiate the reader on the author's particular version of card meanings and interpretation method although we'll necessarily touch on those somewhat. I think it is fair to say the great majority of books written on the Tarot spend most of their time in those two areas. There are already countless resources, including free ones, for that.

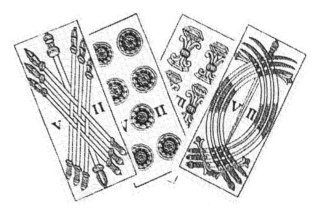

Fig 3 - 7 of Batons, 7 of Coins, 7 of Cups and 7 of Swords.
Composite image made by author of cards
from an 1877 publication.

Still, let's examine and understand the pieces of the deck as a starting point. To begin with we have 4 suits just as with many playing card decks including the ones that were first brought back to Europe by traders, returning soldiers or whoever it may have been. In this case the suits are batons, cups, swords and coins. These mimicked the Islamic suits which were polo sticks, cups, swords and gold coins. Polo sticks became batons/clubs in Europe because that game was unknown there at the time.[11]

Each suit symbol has developed an associated meaning over time and in fact more than one. On top of the qualities each can stand for there is a tradition where each represents an element and a segment of old world society. At a high level, let us say . . .

Batons – fire element – peasantry – willpower, passion, effort, labor

Fig 4 – Batons

Cups – water element – church – emotion, spirituality, healing

Fig 5 – Cups

Swords – air element – nobility – ideas, focus, conflict

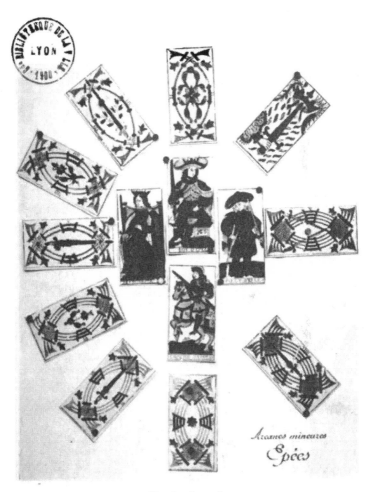

Fig 6 – Swords

Coins – earth element – merchants – resources, treasure, money, possessions

Fig 7 – Coins

Speaking of imposed belief systems, the elemental aspect listed above comes from the near east and subsequent western philosophies. It is unlikely the early card makers or users had that in mind since they were simply copying the suits of the Islamic cards. Just keep in mind as we progress in our story that many see the cards acting as a mirror of sorts for exotic religious-mythological concepts growing in Europe, possibly inherited from earlier societies like Egypt's, Mesopotamia's and India's. And to be fair, the Renaissance was a time when many philosophies outside of the Christian mainstream were being rediscovered, invented and/or embraced.

Back to the deck, each of the 4 suits exists in a set of 14. Each of those sets is then divided into a set of 4, which are the *court cards* (page, knight, queen, king), and a numbered set of 10 called the *minor pips*. Each suit has an Ace card as the '1' of the pips just as with modern playing cards. These 4 sets of 14 form the 56 cards of the minor arcana. There is a baseline commonality of meaning for all the kings just as there is for the queens, etc. However, the King of Cups is very different from the King of Swords and so on. This same duality exists for the minor pips. The 3 of Swords and the 3 of Batons have thematic differences and similarities.

Regardless, those are the 56 cards of the minor arcana. They are joined by the far less systematic and far more mysterious, previously mentioned major arcana. These are a sequence of allegorical, archetypal images that have fascinated many for centuries. Their invention is a complete mystery. They did however spring from the cultural milieu of their birthplace, early Renaissance Italy. The philosophical and artistic explosion beginning to take root was surely a catalyst in the creation of the atouts. Like with so much art of the movement there is much Christian imagery present but more as well. Many see the instances of overtly Christian iconography as stand-ins for more ancient visuals and ideas. Others disagree and in essence argue the opposite, stating that even the pagan images in the major arcana were used to express Christian ideals, a standard artistic practice of the time.

Either way, the revolution of the Renaissance largely came about by looking to the earlier civilizations of Greece and Rome. Doing so broke the European-medieval monolithic fascination with God and elevated man (and woman) as a center of attention. The earlier pantheistic religions with their fractured representations for the self and the forces that influence mortal life also came into the picture, so to speak. We cannot know what ideological filter the original artist(s) had in mind but this is the background that allowed this sequence of images to be created.

Arcanes majeures
Tarot de Marseille

Fig 8 - Here the atouts are arranged in a clockwise manner, from card 0 to 21, totaling 22 images. We will explore the major arcana in detail in Chapter 10.

*   *   *

The cards of the major arcana are a pantheon of their own. They can represent facets of God/the gods, fate and ourselves depending on your outlook. Each is open to multiple interpretations and many, many generations have spent time trying to define them. Maybe God has 22 faces, maybe we are that deity and only wear certain of those faces at certain times. In spite of their humble game roots and the open questions regarding their intentionality, these cards wrestle with the nature of life and existence. *Simply put they are a map of life, the world, and the life of the world.*

There are no suits related to the major arcana. Think of the suits of the minor arcana as four separate kingdoms with their kings, queens, knights and pages but also commoners (the pips). The atouts exist above those earthly realms but rule over and influence them in mysterious ways. This is just as the late medieval, early Renaissance mindset assumed God or the gods to do so in regard to life on Earth.

These 22 were the triumphal cards of the original game. They trumped the lesser cards just as the court cards presumably trumped the pips. Originally the game and cards were called *trionfi* (triumph), later *tarrochi*.[12] The dynamic of some cards triumphing over others was central to the original gameplay but is just as important in understanding the symbolism imbued in the images and the sequence of the major arcana.

Whether game or divination tool, the 3 tier structure (atouts, court, pips) remains. The modern decks based on the Rider-Waite-Smith template change that dynamic somewhat by lavishing visuals on the minor pip cards. I personally prefer the original design where each tier received a different level of visual attention commensurate with the card's symbolic (and gaming) import. However, every revolution produces good and bad effects so there is plenty to enjoy about the modern approach as we'll see.

Whether we're talking traditional or modern, the deck still maps out the same way. 1 set of 22 and 1 set of 56 (4x14). It's important to understand that the 56 is a series of overlapping sets as well. There are 10 series that repeat 4 times each (the minor pips by suit), a series of 14 that repeats 4 times (the entire suits), and a series of 4 that repeats 4 times (the 16 court cards). And each of those is comprised of a series of 4 that repeats 1 time. Meaning there is 1 set of 4 kings, 1 set of 4 queens, etc.

Do not feel like any of that last paragraph needs to be memorized. I just want to get across how complex the deck actually is, and believe me that is only a glimpse. In this book I'd like to do something entirely different from the norm. That is to go ahead and take on the Tarot's ... what to call it ... interdimensional internal structure, specifically through the use of a metaphor.

The only other basic to cover is that reading is done by pulling one or more cards from the shuffled deck. Normally this is done by the reader who is pulling and interpreting cards for the *querent* (also called the *postulant*). This produces a *spread* (*draw*, *hand*) and only the resulting cards are used in the reading. There are countless spread *templates* in existence, each with assorted interpretation values assigned to the cards based on position. A simple example is the *Past, Present, Future* spread made with 3 cards, each of which represents one of those aspects of time (e.g. card on the left is the past, etc.). Cards in a spread do not have to be assigned positional definitions however and some readers actively eschew that kind of finely tuned instruction. Needless to say, each approach has its strengths and weaknesses much like abstract versus traditional art and neither is superior to the other. The bottom line is that the reading processes generally consists of interpreting the cards in light of the question the querent wants to explore.

The Tarot is endlessly fascinating for many people who give it a chance. The unique experiment I'd like to conduct in this work is to flesh out a concrete metaphor for understanding and exploring it. That then gives birth to new exercises for practitioners to try when they use the cards. These exercises can help us better internalize and appreciate just how vast the Tarot's nuances are.

This object and its use has existed for roughly half of millennia and shows no signs of stopping. So why should we not come up with new ways to understand it? Without further ado then, let's begin our archeological and architectural exploration.

We are not just going to delve into how the Tarot is used and what it is used for but also understand the importance of its ritualistic construction and destruction; because that is the art of the Tarot. Reading cards begins with ruins you rebuild, and ends with ruins you leave behind. Doing all of this might provide a new way of understanding this mysterious thing, which is as permanent and rooted is it is ever-changing.

CHAPTER 3

SACRED PLACES,
SACRED THINGS

"The other statues, those of monsters and demons, had no hatred for him – he resembled them too closely for that. It was rather the rest of mankind that they jeered at. The saints were his friends and blessed him; the monsters were his friends and kept watch over him. He would sometimes spend whole hours crouched before one of the statues in solitary conversation with it." *The Hunchback of Notre Dame* 1831[13]

BEFORE PROCEEDING I have to break my original narrative to point out that it was during the editing phase of this book's creation, and the *same day* that I had finished revising musings on medieval church fires no less, that the magnificent Notre Dame Cathedral was engulfed in a horrific fire. I walked away from completing said revisions and returned to see the cultural tragedy unfolding on television. As you'll find, that building is a touchstone of sorts in this book and I pray it is fully restored or well on its way by the time you read these words.

*   *   *

Humans have tried to imagine the abodes of the gods and their inhabitants since time immemorial. One version has a cloudy heaven in the sky fronted by pearly gates. The Greeks looked to the mountaintop of Olympus here on Earth. The Hindu religion has Mt. Meru, a golden (by some descriptions) mountain that is the axis of the world and so large that the Himalayas are its foothills.

And just as often as different societies tried to picture these places and their occupants, they built temples and monuments to them. The globe is littered with them and they of course include the churches, synagogues, mosques and temples that are actively used around the world today. This impulse then is just as active now as it ever was. Entering such a structure separates the visitor from the more mundane earthly locations and cares. They acted, and act today, as portals to other realms.

An additional note is that none of this was restricted to heavenly character traits or abodes. The Vikings imagined Asgard as a loftier, grander version of the kingly halls and lands populating the Earth (Midgard) but there was also the lands of the dwarves, ice giants, the dead, etc. in that Scandinavian cosmos. As our opening quotation reminds us, even Christian holy places didn't just show holy things. Demons and gargoyles are often enshrined in stone along with the more angelic beings.

What links the various heavens and hells from practically all cultures that have ever existed is that they imagined these places and then built holy sites in honor of or deference to them. So, ziggurats, temples and monuments were constructed the world over. It is perhaps the universal object built to honor, connect to and try to understand the divine. But it isn't the only one.

Humans have also built small religious objects that they could take anywhere with them. A cross around the neck, a Native American's medicine bag, etc. The examples are endless. So we have two dueling but not mutually exclusive traditions . . . things that are built and things that are carried. Technically of course the small objects are built as well but I think it's clear what we mean. The things that are built are sacred spaces that you step up to or in to. Notre Dame does not go to you, you go to it. The things carried allow users to tune out the distractions around them regardless of where they are. A Muslim using a prayer rug at the right time of day, regardless of location, is an example of this practice.

The remarkable thing about Tarot cards is how well they invoke both of these traditions. If you recall, earlier in the book we borrowed the phrase nomadic cathedral. That is a fantastic description of the Tarot deck. It is a handheld object that you take with you but it creates a unique place of worship or meditation around you when used. At least, that is the contention of this work.

In other words, a spread of the cards creates a church of a kind. It can invoke several of the 22 gods or just one. Its structures, walls, pillars and windows change depending on how many cards are drawn and which cards they happen to be. Imagine the deck as an architectural talisman. It is a conjuring implement whose results can be thought of as a physical structure although one does not actually result from the ritual.

In a Catholic church you will find one or more deities elevated above the rest. Usually Jesus will have the premier place, at the apse, but Mary and Joseph may have statues flanking the altar. Their important but secondary location would be higher than that afforded to various saints depicted elsewhere in the building. These things are not always arranged in the same order. The Virgin Mary may have a special location in one, giving her an exclusive status second only to Christ. Sometimes she even occupies center stage as it were. Meanwhile a church named after a particular saint will have a special accommodation for that figure. All of this happens through a combination of statues, stained glass windows and various other features on the inside. On the outside, think of the previously mentioned Notre Dame.

* * *

Fig 9 - Notre Dame in the days of yore.

This medieval masterpiece is a multi-sectioned wonder. The towers reach up to heaven while on the bottom, 3 different entrances allow mortals to enter into the sacred space. Each entrance is dedicated to a different divine figure or event. They are the Portal of the Last Judgment (center), the Portal of the Virgin (Left) and the Portal of St. Anne (South). In between the bottom and the top there are sections with biblical scenes, angels and more. There is the Gallery of Kings but also the Gallery of Chimeras so earthly rulers and magical creatures are both present. And yes, there are everyday people, at least in the form of sinners looking for redemption.

Those already familiar with Tarot cards, especially the older versions, may find that list of features quite familiar. Standing in front of this Paris landmark provides more than the eye or mind can take in at once given all the elements at play. But, I would say that is appropriate given the challenge of trying to carve one structure that takes in the many faceted mystery that is the godhead. So you could stand in front of the cathedral and meditate on just one of the many scenes or even minor characters carved in front of you. The next day or moment you could focus elsewhere. Walking inside would add to your choices.

Now think of how even just the houses of worship in one religion change from one building to the next much less from one religion to the next. Finally imagine trying to design an artifact that captures this cosmic complexity. That artifact would show you just one aspect, or a select few, of the vast possibilities. Also, it would show you a different aspect or aspects every time you use it. You probably know where we're going with this. I believe you'd find it impossible to create something that could do all of that better than the Tarot already does.

And it does that by combining the two major categories of worship objects we discussed. It is the cross, the rosary, the prayer rug, etc. that allows a person to separate themselves from the world wherever they happen to be sitting. They contemplate the eternal instead of the temporal in the bubble they've created. But unlike the prayer aides just mentioned, the Tarot gives structure to the temporary space. Think of it as creating a temple on the spot because, just like a real temple, it has a limited structure but in the best possible sense. It focuses your attention on a certain saint, god, force or a specific combination of them. And still there is more.

One specific type of sacred place was an oracle, most famously the Greek Oracle at Delphi. Seekers would go to such places to ask their questions. The answer was, however, rarely straightforward. In 480 BCE the Persians were carving a path towards Athens. This resulted after the legendary stand of the Spartans at Thermopylae. In such a dire situation they naturally turned to the famed oracle for guidance on how to resist the coming invasion.

> "Though all else shall be taken . . . Yet Zeus, the all-seeing grants to Athena's prayer that the wooden wall only shall not fall."[14]

Furious debate ensued about what the advice actually meant but it was finally decided that it referred to the Athenian navy. This in fact turned out to be the mechanism for the salvation of Athens and that was that. The fact that an oracular answer is somewhat ambiguous should apply to Tarot readings and does for many readers. Additionally there is the fact that a draw of even just one card can be taken in multiple different ways.

That then was one form of interpreting guidance from above but an oracle did not have to be a site. There was no need to travel if you had a priest, soothsayer, etc. with you who could perform a roaming ritual. The flight of birds, entrails of sacrificed animals and countless other methods were used for these purposes.

And once again our 78 cards do a fine job of synthesizing multiple traditions. They provide the simulated location/ structure as discussed along with the transportable artifact. If you can't go to Delphi, bring it with you. And this touches much more directly on the Tarot's use than does the church, synagogue, etc. Use of the cards for divination came along long after the heyday of similar practices but it is still in use today. And to be honest, houses of worship may have overtaken those of outright divination but the former are really still used as the latter. After all, how many people walk into churches and the like in this day and age and pray for answers to their specific questions, or for a sign to help them navigate a trying situation?

It would be impressive enough if Tarot cards continued the many traditions this chapter covers, and it does, so it is. However, our roving oracular temple cum personal prayer object incorporates more and it once again does so accidentally.

Buddhist monks from Tibet and elsewhere create magnificent visual representations of life, death, divine forces and the rest of the great questions. These *mandalas* are intricate designs which are meticulously made in various ways. The quintessential version is done with millions of grains of colored sand. A quick online search would be infinitely justified if the reader is not already familiar with these works of spirituality and art. Each of them can be thought of as a spirit atlas. Like the cards, they express the complexities of being and existence through a visual language. The benefits of this approach are not just that you have something beautiful to behold, but that the creator can convey so much in so little space. In other words, spread all the pages of the Bible or Koran across a floor and the result will take up far more space than our 78 cards or a mandala. The thematic links between mandalas and the Tarot are strong enough that writer, filmmaker and Tarot guru Alejandro Jodorowsky made it his mission to create a mandala out of the entire deck as part of his exploration of the Tarot.[15]

So the cards speak visually, the same as a Tibetan mandala, the face of Notre Dame or the collection of immense Nazca line drawings in Peru for that matter. But they also do something only the Buddhist artifact does compared to those other two. Cathedrals last all but forever and the lines in Peru can still be seen. A sand mandala though, is destroyed by the same monks who create it. Watching the erasing of such an exquisite work is wince inducing but the impermanence of everything is paid homage to by this act. The sands are collected and then dropped into a river so that they may flow back into the world as a blessing. Mandalas are therefore forever created and destroyed, a cyclical ritual very different from the need to build permanent monuments like temples or pyramids. I'm sure you see the association that comes up for our purposes. The temple built by creating a spread of cards is always destroyed, only to be later rebuilt.

We could jump to Japan for a large scale example of this all. Well there's no could to it, we will, if only briefly. Emphasis added . . .

"Every 20 years, locals tear down the Ise Jingu grand shrine in Mie Prefecture, Japan, only to rebuild it anew. They have been doing this for around 1,300 years . . . This is an important national event. Its underlying concept – that *repeated rebuilding renders sanctuaries eternal* – is unique in the world."[16]

The building in question is made of wood. This material obviously wears away much faster than stone or metal. Yet by continually rebuilding it with fresh lumber, the Japanese ironically preserve the original better than if it were made of sturdier materials which would show their age despite their sturdiness. Put simply, the shrine always looks as it did 1,300 years ago when it was new.

The repeated rebuilding of the Tarot's shrine also renders an eternal sanctuary. If an ancient stone church is destroyed it is, sadly, lost forever. Not so with the deck that can always be reprinted.

We've seen that religious objects are sometimes small and therefore portable. Conversely they can be large and permanent but also purposefully impermanent in some cases. Well what about large and portable? This improbable combination also exists, notably in the Torah and Bible. According to Jewish tradition, the *tabernacle* (*Mishkan*, or place of divine dwelling in Hebrew) was a portable temple built after the flight from Egypt and used to commune with God during the 40 year journey from Egypt to the Holy Land. This was a small complex; an enclosure formed an outer yard which contained the temple as it were, a large tent (the Tent of Meeting). Inside that, an arrangement of furniture and objects dictated to Moses by God himself was arranged. Screened by curtains was the innermost space, the Holy of Holies, which contained the Ark of the Covenant. The entire complex was, "A portable sanctuary in the wilderness"[17] and adds yet another variation to ways humanity carried the gods with them, or reached out to them. It also reminds us of the cards as the cards remind us of it.

The Tarot deck taps into an ever present impulse, the desire to understand the existential mysteries by creating a physical object that captures, or fractures, its facets. It is underappreciated just how adroitly it does that regardless of its original intention. As seen it even mimics the underlying principles of many pre-existing traditions from around the world . . . large, small, common and uncommon. This object manages to touch on countless sacred places, countless sacred things.

CHAPTER 4

THE PLATONIC TEMPLE

"In his Socratic dialogues Plato argues through Socrates that because the material world is changeable it is also unreliable. But Plato also believed that this is not the whole story. Behind this unreliable world of appearances is a world of permanence and reliability. Plato calls this more real (because permanent) world, the world of 'Forms' or 'Ideas' (*eidos/idea* in Greek)." *Philosophy Now: A Magazine of Ideas*[18]

To make things official then, we will be exploring the Tarot by envisioning it as a temple of sorts, but one that is different each time it is constructed. It can be made anywhere and is destroyed after each use. The building is done through the use of the talismanic deck, which acts as a library of ever changing blueprints. The reader never knows which design will be employed until the spread is complete and the prayer or meditation receives structure based on that of the fleeting creation. The exercise is therefore simultaneously the same and different every time.

We saw in our last chapter how that is a practice that touches on many others throughout human history. The cards were probably not consciously designed for this purpose which makes our oracle as improbable as it is accidental. And yet it is just as profound as those that were purpose built. In fact, its original agnostic outlook may have been a secret strength. By not being tied to any one belief system, a more open and versatile ritual was allowed to develop over the centuries. That is true even if the allegory in the major arcana was consciously Christian. It was after all just a game and not a religious tool. Over the centuries various beliefs have organically become a part of Tarot tradition but users only incorporate the ones they find productive.

* * *

Frenchman, Protestant pastor and Freemason Antoine Court de Gébelin (Born 1719) famously encountered the cards being used by foreigners, the game having fallen into disuse amongst his countrymen. In his large 9 volume work, *Monde Primitif* (*The Primitive World*, 1783), he briefly touched on the Tarot, stating unequivocally that the cards were a forgotten relic from the religion and wisdom of ancient Egypt. The mythical Book of Thoth was claimed as the Tarot's ancestor; its wisdom preserved for the ages in the symbolism of the cards.

> "But this game's form, disposition and arrangement and its trumps are so magnificently allegorical and these allegories are so congruent with the ancient Egypt's civil, philosophical and religious doctrines that we can only identify this work as that of these wise people: only they could have been its inventor."[19]

> "The Egyptian game Tarot, on the other hand, is well suited for divination as it somehow represents the entire

universe and the various matters affecting the human condition."[20]

To be clear, there is absolutely no evidence to support the ancient Egyptian connection but the idea was highly influential nonetheless. Look back to the opening quotation of Chapter 1 to see how it was alive and well in practically the 20th century. It still persists in some quarters. It is however ironic that cards overall were likely introduced to Europe from contemporary Egypt. Regardless, if you remove the word, "Egyptian" from the 2nd quotation above then Gébelin gives an excellent description of the Tarot or at least how it can be used. In fact he was far more prophetic than he could have imagined when he talked about the, "universe" but we'll return to that in Chapter 6.

Gébelin's hypothesis staked the claim regarding thoughts on an esoteric origin for the Tarot even if it was just one small piece of a larger work. It is likely the first and surely the most famous of the early steps in the tradition of grafting whatever belief systems seemed appropriate into the interpretation of the Tarot.

He was followed almost immediately by another French occultist, Jean-Baptiste Alliette (Born 1738), who's pen name was Etteilla. He essentially invented Tarot cartomancy. This included writing the first book dedicated to using tarot cards for divination, creating his own deck and popularizing many conventions that are still a part of tarot orthodoxy. Part of his approach was linking the cards to astrology, a union that is unquestioned by most to this very day.

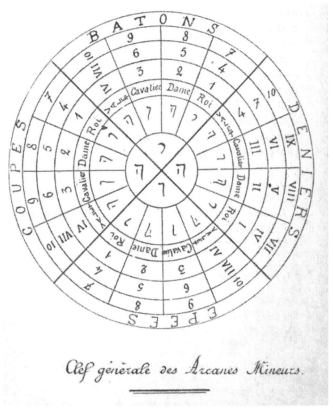

Clef générale des Arcanes Mineurs.

Fig 10 - Many novel charts and graphs such as this were created over the last few centuries to bridge the gap between the organization of the Tarot deck and the claim that it was created based on a mystical belief system.

The versatility of the cards shines through in both cases however because this kind of philosophical scavenging can work. The archetypal structure and images captured in our early Renaissance artifact are drawn from the same well of the collective unconscious as any religion or mythology, giving the cards the connection points needed or looked for by various parties to suit their purposes. At least that would be the Jungian explanation of the Tarot's applicability and adaptability. There will be more to say on Carl Jung as this will be approximately the umpteenth time someone associates his thoughts with the Tarot.

To return to our transitory temple however we need to go back to far earlier than Jung in the history of Western thought. This thinker is a founding father of philosophy and was born in Athens circa 427 BCE. Our chapter's opening quotation leaves no mystery as to the philosopher in question. We are talking about Plato, the student of Socrates and teacher of Aristotle. In particular the concept of the *platonic forms* relates strongly to our temple metaphor.

Plato taught that there is an ideal version of things which no physical specimen can match. We can encounter various examples of objects but for each of them there exists in our soul an abstract version that the real world specimens only imitate.

What if every spread drawn was similarly a fragmented piece or partial view of the Tarot's platonic form? To be clear we're only imagining this as a mental exercise for understanding the Tarot. We are extending our metaphor to include a comprehensive, multifaceted structure. It's a building that encompasses all of the Tarot's many aspects; the suits, the numbers, the courts, the major arcana, the 4 sets of 4, the 4 sets of 14, etc.

It would be a stone chimera because it would have so many different parts and features. It could be part Notre Dame, ziggurat, mosque, palace, Native American estufa (underground holy place), Buddhist monastery and anything else that works in the mind of the one doing the imagining.

Our castle isn't just a static hybrid either. It is a polymorph, an object that changes shape. Imagine then this immense, morphing castle standing alone in a distant land. The reader can never reach it but by using the cards creates a small, partial emulation of it. The actual structure is so large and complex that it would be overwhelming to step inside of it or try to take in visually from the outside. But it is beautiful nonetheless with countless, differently shaped towers and spires, outer and inner walls, courtyards, levels and more.

Thinking of 22 gods or forces, four kingdoms, etc. all at once would not be productive. Casting a spread allows you to focus on a manageable number of aspects, so that the exercise of reading can be productive.

Earlier we talked about how the Tarot deck has been continually reimagined in the postmodern era. This is yet another reason why our castle-cathedral can take on different looks.

If you cast the cards with a deck that has a theme of nature then the imaginary space you step into would be naturally . . . well, natural. It could be a wooded enclosure, lit by the Sun or Moon.

If you were using an Egyptian themed deck then your structure will clearly have that motif throughout. And so on and so on. I've talked more than once about the Tarot's versatility so our castle in the sky (or whatever it may be) needs to be adaptable as well.

And it isn't as if decor is the only thing that changes. It is that but also a question of what parts of the great castle make it into your temporary version. I read a spread using a deck I was unfamiliar with which had the nature theme alluded to above. The Emperor was a large majestic tree with the Sun shining above it in the sky. The Seven of Clubs was one torch surrounded by six unlit ones and the card was reversed. The other two cards in this where the Sun (also reversed) and the Star.

I imagined a druidic-like place of worship. It was night

because there was a star (the Star card that is) in the sky and the Sun was upside down. And when you stand on a part of the Earth that is experiencing night, the Sun is upside down relative to your vantage point. Things are never simple with the Tarot though so a large, majestic tree in the center somehow had sunlight focused on it and it alone, thanks to the Emperor card's visuals. The Star shined in the otherwise dark sky. Something like this can happen in a magical place so there it was. Meanwhile the only light on the ground outside of the tree's solar spotlight was provided by the one lit torch.

I imagined all of this as being inside our castle. It was a cavernous space. The floor was grass and the surroundings so dark and distant that it was no different from being outdoors. The Sun and star shown through openings in the imperceptible ceiling.

In this example 2 of the 22 faces of God were present (e.g. major arcana cards). In more of a medieval church-like space they could have been two large stained glass windows, one at each end of the church or two statues sharing the altar.

All of that was a simple example. Creating it was intuitive, fun and much more immersive than just looking at the cards. Now imagine a spread like the above but with a court card in the mix. How would that be represented in our space? And what of the number four? After all, that's how many cards were in the spread. Is that the number of walls containing the space or some other feature?

Unfortunately it took many words to describe something that took seconds to imagine. You can paint a mental picture infinitely faster than you can describe it to someone else. Anyway, this then is the concept the book is built around in practice. The art of reading the cards has been continually reinvented for centuries. For instance someone, somewhere, is no doubt creating a brand new spread template as you read this sentence. The Tarot's original users surely never imagined a *starting a business spread* but it exists today. A few writers have recommended visualizing a card, mentally stepping into it so to speak but that is apparently the only experiment that even approaches ours. The point is, the evolution continues so perhaps this book's technique can help us expand our understanding just as other innovations have.

For a medium which is almost entirely visual it does make sense to use a visual methodology to explore it. Forcing yourself to create your own cohesive mental construct based on the images of the randomly chosen cards seems almost natural in retrospect.

And, like all the other lore out there, the reader is free to use as much or as little of this as they like. Sometimes I will make a conscious effort to create the imaginary building in great detail. But other times it is just a fleeting, transient thing . . . a building whose features are barely discernible, like one you walked through during a dream.

CHAPTER 5

ARCHETYPES, ARCHES AND ARCHEOLOGY

"... so far as the collective unconscious contents are concerned we are dealing with archaic or—I would say—primordial types, that is, with universal images that have existed since the remotest times." Carl Jung[21]

"In contrast, the middle period dialogues are thought to present the views of Plato, though nonetheless Socrates remains the speaker. Here for the first time we find remarks about the immortality of the soul, about special entities called 'Forms' that exist outside of space and time and that are both the objects of knowledge and somehow the cause of whatever transpires in the physical world, and the doctrine of recollection, the thesis that the immortal soul, in a disembodied state prior to its incarceration in a body, viewed these Forms, knowledge of which is then recalled by incarcerated souls through a laborious process." *Plato's Middle Period Metaphysics and Epistemology*[22]

W E BRIEFLY MENTIONED Carl Jung and how he has been associated with the Tarot before now. If the Tarot has a modern and scientific justification then it comes from him. He is the modern master that joins Plato in creating the philosophical and intellectual principles that our mystical structure is built upon. But that is not to say someone has to subscribe to his teachings, or anyone else's, to effectively use the cards.

Still, a physical building needs to be based on sound principles of mathematics and physics or it won't stand for very long. To provide penetrating insights to its users, the cards have to likewise leverage the workings of the human mind, and perhaps soul.

It is no accident that Jung's influential thoughts about the psyche and humanity have been much cited in regard to the Tarot. There are even whole books dedicated to the correlation. Jung himself was never a devotee of the cards but did speak positively about them and even commissioned experiments with them and other divinatory tools.[23]

Originally Jung wanted to be an archeologist. An archeologist in part maps out the archaic remains of what humanity built in the past. Those buildings and their designs tell us about the people who built them, they are physical reflections of their thoughts on life, the gods and themselves. Jung brought a similar approach to psychology. The ancient remains he discovered and mapped out ended up existing in the human mind instead of on or under the ground. And because we carry those ruins within ourselves they still have a profound effect today. So the insights to be had are not just about the original builders but also us, their distant descendants.

*   *   *

At a high-level, Jung defined three different realms of the psyche . . .

- The conscious mind
- The personal unconscious
- The collective unconscious

The conscious mind is all but self-explanatory for our superficial overview. Each person encounters a unique set of stimuli every day and actively (e.g. consciously) processes/ keeps much of it. The personal unconscious is also unique to each individual as its name implies. This is partially what comes out in your dreams, etc. The thoughts, memories and feelings buried beneath your conscious mind that came from your direct experiences are the essence of this category. Both of those are fairly intuitive for anyone to grasp, at least for our purposes. Then however we get to a revolution in the understanding of humanity.

The collective unconscious is a pool of universally shared and accessed patterns and images. They are archaic in origin as they reach deep into prehistory. Jung classified these patterns as *archetypes*. If his thoughts on the workings of the mind were correct, then that would help explain the occurrences of many archetypes throughout history in completely different cultures, religions and mythologies. It would also be why some character and story templates like the famous hero's journey are so persistent. Jung formulated his theory based on comparative religion and mythology as well as his work treating individual patients so he saw these recurrent patterns from the individual to the societal level. One thing that is very important to note for our study is that these are accessed and triggered visually. Symbols are of great importance in Jungian psychology. We connect to these archaic underpinnings of ourselves visually. As one Jungian professor noted, "Symbols are that which guide psychological development... You cannot *not* react to a symbol."[24]

Ultimately, this would all play into the innate hold archetypal images like those on the cards have on us. Consciousness is on the surface, the personal unconscious is below that, the collective unconscious lies beneath even that. So seeing an authentic archetypal visage taps into the deepest layer of our psyche according to this theory.

Plato's thoughts and Jung's are not exactly the same but we can see the similarities. Both of these intellectual giants reasoned that archetypal concepts have a profound impact on us and that our minds instinctively reach for them. Each person can decide how literally they want to take the concept of these things existing outside of our actual selves. If you believe in a greater power then it would be natural for that spirit to be the source of these things. If however there is nothing to any religion or philosophy outside of what exists in our brain's neural networks, the concept does not actually change. In that scenario, only the 'location' of the forms, the archetypes, does.

And this is one of the Tarot's greatest strengths; it works well regardless of an individual's cosmological view. Each of us carries those deeper, harder to access levels of thought; ideas and the idealized. It is beneficial to have a way to keep in tune with them. Jung felt a healthy exchange between the layers of consciousness was necessary for the operation of a healthy psyche. A state of equilibrium via give and take has to be established and that is something the 78 cards can facilitate. A usual reading involves focusing on a particular question or problem. The epiphanies often experienced by the person asking the question are realizations of thoughts on the matter but thoughts that were previously inaccessible to them. And at the risk of re-emphasizing a point, the origins of those revelations can be believed to be of strictly human origin or not. Either way, the cards offer a specific way to perform a symbol based exercise that helps us better stay in tune with those thoughts or messages.

Don't forget that our temple is a shapeshifter though so it can even match the mind of the person entering it instead of them needing to match their minds to it. In other words, a Catholic church's imagery speaks specifically to its intended visitors through the shared tenets of that faith. Each religion, mythology, etc. translates the universal contents of the collective unconscious into modified versions.

> "Primitive tribal lore is concerned with archetypes that have been modified in a special way. They are no longer contents of the unconscious, but have already been changed into conscious formulae taught according to tradition ... Another well-known expression of the archetypes is myth and fairytale. But there too we are dealing with forms that have received a specific stamp and have been handed down." *The Archetypes and the Collective Unconscious Carl Jung Volume 9, Part I*[25]

The Tarot's dialogue via visual language is a bit more open than most because it doesn't subscribe to just one dogma's optic interpretation of the universal, at least not as it has been used and recreated for a long time now.

The freedom to be remade into an ever growing population of variations is why the person looking to acquire their first deck is often told to choose whichever set of imagery resonates with them. Granted the kitschier decks lose much of the archetypal connection. Cards full of cartoon kittens may be fun but likely do not help us enter those prehistoric ruins in our mind. Likewise there is no guarantee that a modern artist drawing their own cards, even in a serious way, will connect to the archetypes meaningfully. Furthermore it could be argued that the modern penchant for lavishing images on every card muddies the waters, or dilutes our connection to the true archetypes whereas the traditional approach was more focused and therefore connected since only the atouts received such treatment. Then again a strength could be that 78 paintings equals that many more chances to hit upon a template that strongly impacts a viewer.

*   *   *

The important thinkers who can inform our understanding of what the Tarot does doesn't stop with Plato and Jung. If anything they are the philosophical bookends. Between them are other figures of importance.

> "In the universe, there are things that are known, and things that are unknown, and in between, there are doors." William Blake[26]

Our temple has many doors but is itself one, a door to the unknown within us. We temporarily move outside of the temporal and connect more with what Blake called the *infinite* when we step through the portal created by the cards.

Immanuel Kant (born 1724) established a similar concept to the forms, what he called the *thing-in-itself*.

> "And we indeed, rightly considering objects of sense as mere appearances, confess thereby that they are based upon a thing in itself, though we know not this thing as it is in itself, but only know its appearances, viz., the way in which our senses are affected by this unknown something." *Prolegomena*[27]

All of this may sound vaguely eastern and for good reason. Arthur Schopenhauer (born 1788) was influenced by Hindu and Buddhist thought. Incorporating the concept that the world we experience is essentially an illusion into his philosophy, he saw the similarity that the thoughts of Kant and others had with this notion. Practice of the Tarot does not require one to believe the world is illusory but the idea of truer, conceptual-archetypal things helps us understand how images like the Tarot's work on our minds as we think through given situations or just visually meditate.

And the biggest surprise may be that all of this works in a very real, practical way. Engaging in visual discourse with the forms presented by our temporary church encourages deeper than conscious level thoughts to rise to the surface. And this helpful ritual is repeated throughout a lifetime of Tarot reading just as Tibetan monks always build more mandalas and the Japanese keep rebuilding their shrine. Aristotle wasn't talking about the yet to be invented Tarot but might as well have been when he said, ". . . we are what we repeatedly do. Excellence then, is not an act, but a habit."[28]

The Tarot's originators were surely as unpreoccupied with Plato and Aristotle as they were unaware that the fields of psychology and comparative mythology would be created in a few centuries. Their creation however connects with important traditions in Western and even global thought about the nature of existence. These then are some of the principles that make the temporary temple's structures sound and allow its use to remain enduring.

CHAPTER 6

OF COMBINATIONS AND PERMUTATIONS

"Number is the ruler of forms and ideas, and the cause of gods and daemons." *Life of Pythagoras*[29]

"All is number" Motto of the Pythagorean School[30]

THE RAISON D'ÊTRE for this whole book is that the interlocking complexities of the Tarot are far too labyrinthine to encapsulate but should still be appreciated. This inherent vastness is frankly underexplored and this in turn is probably because the task is so daunting.

To that end, let's put a fine point on proving we're not overstating the vastness contained within the Tarot's simple 78 cards. In fact, remember how Pythagoras, Gébelin and Blake all used the word universe in earlier chapters? That is appropriate as we have to think on that scale if we dare to delve into just how vast the totals within our Pandora's Box of 78 cards really are.

Blake talked about the doors to the unknown things in the universe and we in turn talked about how the Tarot itself is one of those doors, or a portal containing many doors. Strange to say but you're about to imagine more doors than you ever have. And as you're about to see, Gébelin was accurate when he said the cards can represent the universe itself. Lastly, Pythagoras stated that if we know ourselves, then we'll know the universe and God (quoted later in this book).

The Tarot is a method of self-discovery first and foremost. And yet it does in fact get us a bit closer to grasping the universe and a bit closer to understanding God, whatever that is, for the same reason Pythagoras made that last statement of his.

Pythagoras wasn't just a historically brilliant mathematician, he was also a great classical philosopher. He saw numbers as the key to understanding everything. Having traveled and studied as far east as Babylon, he could be considered the father of numerology in western civilization. He likely brought back the notion that numbers inherently represent things beyond the physical and to the spiritual, and then expanded on that concept with his supra-genius intellect. So, let's leave no stone unturned in following his lead when it comes to our subject.

Combinations

How many different 1 card spreads can be drawn from a standard deck? 78 is the obvious answer. And whenever you pull a single card you know that you only had a 1 in 78 chance of that happening. What if you use all 78 cards in a spread (this has been designed and done by the way)? Well there's little mystery here too; you can only ever draw the same 78 cards. How many different sets of cards are available in between those two extremes though? The answer is sure to surprise you.

The *Celtic Cross* is one of the most common spreads used today. It utilizes 10 cards. So how many unique 10 card combinations can be drawn from the total 78? Would you believe 1,258,315,963,905? That's right, the odds of getting whatever unique set of 10 cards you happen to draw are about 1 in 1.3 trillion. It is difficult for us to even fathom that figure.

CNN tried to help its readers understand the enormity of 1 trillion dollars. They did this by calculating that if you'd begun with that amount at the birth of Jesus Christ and began spending 1 million dollars every single day, you would still not be out of money. You could essentially use that spread (or any 10 card draw) for eternity and never get a repeat. Alejandro Jodorowsky teaches a circle pattern spread using 24 cards.[31] There are 79,065,487,387,985,398,300 unique card combinations that can be had that way. That is in the quintillions, an absurd scale to even try and comprehend. But if you'd like to try, know that what astronomers consider our local group of galaxies form an area that is 62 quintillion kilometers wide.

Smaller spreads manage to stay in more earthly realms but the variety is still impressive. 3,003 unique combinations can be explored with 2 card draws. 76,076 combinations result when you add just 1 more to the mix. And you only have to get to the 4's to break the one million mark. And that breaks the threshold quite easily as a 4 card hand results in 1.4 million variations.

Let's see the entire universe of possible outcomes dictated by the number of cards drawn. The expansion and contraction of totals forms an elegant parabola with so many untold millions that it is worth taking in even if we can't truly grasp the enormity of it all. And really, how many people have spent a lifetime with the cards and never realized or appreciated this?

Granted there aren't spreads that commonly use more than say 30 cards. Still, the symmetry and volume available in the entire deck is magnificent and surely worth mapping out fully, perhaps for the first time ever.

"Then I was given a long cane like a measuring rod, and I was told, 'Get up and measure God's sanctuary'" Book of Revelation 11:1[32]

Combinations . . .

Number of cards:	Totals:
1	78
2	3,003
3	76,076
4	1,426,425
5	21,111,090
6	256,851,595
7	2,641,902,120
8	23,446,881,315
9	182,364,632,450
10	1,258,315,963,905
11	7,778,680,504,140
12	43,430,966,148,115
13	220,495,674,290,430
14	1,023,729,916,348,425
15	4,367,914,309,753,280
16	17,198,662,594,653,540
17	62,724,534,168,736,440
18	212,566,476,905,162,380
19	671,262,558,647,881,200
20	1,980,224,548,011,249,540
21	5,469,191,608,792,974,920
22	14,170,178,259,145,435,020
23	34,501,303,587,484,537,440
24	79,065,487,387,985,398,300
25	170,781,452,758,048,460,328
26	348,131,422,929,868,015,284
27	670,475,333,050,116,177,584
28	1,221,222,928,055,568,752,028
29	2,105,556,772,509,601,296,600
30	3,439,076,061,765,682,117,780
31	5,325,020,998,862,991,666,240
32	7,821,124,592,080,019,009,790
33	10,902,173,673,808,511,346,980
34	14,429,347,509,452,441,488,650
35	18,139,751,154,740,212,157,160
36	21,666,924,990,384,142,298,830
37	24,594,887,826,922,539,906,780
38	26,536,589,497,469,056,215,210
39	27,217,014,869,199,000,000,000
40	26,536,589,497,469,056,215,210
41	24,594,887,826,922,539,906,780
42	21,666,924,990,384,142,298,830
43	18,139,751,154,740,212,157,160
44	14,429,347,509,452,441,488,650
45	10,902,173,673,808,511,346,980
46	7,821,124,592,080,019,009,790
47	5,325,020,998,862,991,666,240
48	3,439,076,061,765,682,117,780
49	2,105,556,772,509,601,296,600
50	1,221,222,928,055,568,752,028
51	670,475,333,050,116,177,584
52	348,131,422,929,868,015,284
53	170,781,452,758,048,460,328
54	79,065,487,387,985,398,300
55	34,501,303,587,484,537,440
56	14,170,178,259,145,435,020
57	5,469,191,608,792,974,920
58	1,980,224,548,011,249,540
59	671,262,558,647,881,200
60	212,566,476,905,162,380
61	62,724,534,168,736,440
62	17,198,662,594,653,540
63	4,367,914,309,753,280
64	1,023,729,916,348,425
65	220,495,674,290,430
66	43,430,966,148,115
67	7,778,680,504,140
68	1,258,315,963,905
69	182,364,632,450
70	23,446,881,315
71	2,641,902,120
72	256,851,595
73	21,111,090
74	1,426,425
75	76,076
76	3,003
77	78
78	1

Fig 11 - Combinations

In our last chapter we spoke of the philosophical and psychological underpinnings that the Tarot method is constructed upon and compared it to the mathematical principles a sound physical structure is designed around. As we see above, mathematics has its place within the Tarot as well. Yes it would be fair to call this an accidental complexity; appropriate enough for an accidental oracle. No one had this in mind during the deck's invention or evolution. As far as I know, no one has ever even captured these numbers, or measurements of our temple if you will, until now. And no, they are not needed to read the cards but I hope you'll take time to plumb the depths offered here.

There are innumerable surprises to be had. Regarding symmetry, who knew there are as many 3 card combinations in the deck as there are 75 card combinations or as many 4 card combinations as there are 74 card hands, etc.? Perhaps someone with a Ph.D. in mathematics but not me. And keep in mind every number we see in our table is unique. The 76,076 hands that can be drawn by 4 cards are different from the 76,076 that can be had with sets of 75. That may sound obvious but the repetition of numbers can mislead us into not realizing that we would need to add up all of the numbers in our 2nd column to find the total number of unique combinations available in the Tarot. Despite the trivial nature of all of this knowledge, it is satisfying to know. For instance, when pulling 6 cards there is an inherent value in understanding that there are over <u>256 million</u> possibilities of which you are experiencing just 1.

Similarly, you probably never wondered what sized draw gives you the largest possible number of combinations but why not know that the answer is 39 cards? Those 39 give you more than 27 sextillion spreads. How best to rationalize that amount in our minds? Consider that there are *only* around 1 sextillion stars in all of the <u>known universe</u>.[33] Until running the numbers above I certainly never thought of creating a 39 card draw but now feel compelled to at least once, just to know I tapped into that multitude.

Well we teased how you could compute the absolute total number of hands available from the deck and we can't pass up that opportunity now can we? If you add up all of the figures in the 2nd column of our table, the answer tips the scales at beyond 302 sextillion. *So if nothing else, remember that the 78 cards of the Tarot contain approximately 300 times more combinations than there are stars in the entire universe.*

It should now be apparent why it is a chimerical cathedral that the cards invoke. That imaginary inventory of columns, windows, statutes, towers, steps, altars, etc. needs to be combinable into a breathtaking variety of configurations. The morphing never ends and the fractal versions of it created by the cards each time are all true, all perfect in their own way. The extent of the variety exposed in this chapter is why the ritual is repetitive but never redundant. We are only ever seeing the most imperceptibly small fraction of the total building we talked about earlier. In fact a lifetime of pulling cards doesn't even begin to explore a noticeable portion of our living monument.

It would be more than enough if the numbers we've reviewed were the extent of the cards' depths but it is not. In fact it's not even close. There are common conventions in Tarot reading that explode the already unfathomable extent of the number ranges above.

Reversals- Many choose to interpret a reversed (e.g. upside down) card differently than when it is in its usual orientation. If you subscribe to that method then there are really 156 total cards in the Tarot but only 78 of which you get to hold at once. I prefer keeping to the traditional 78 if you will but regardless, the reversed meanings are often employed. Adding this nuance does far more than double our totals.

Here are the combinations that come out of having 156 potential cards.

Combinations with Reversals . . .

Number of Cards:	Totals:
1	156
2	12,090
3	620,620
4	23,738,715
5	721,656,936
6	18,181,699,556
7	389,179,276,200
8	7,248,464,019,225
9	119,196,963,871,700
10	1,752,195,368,913,990
11	23,256,411,260,131,100
12	281,014,969,393,251,000
13	3,112,761,198,432,930,000
14	31,794,836,537,064,900,000
15	300,991,119,217,548,000,000
16	2,652,484,238,104,640,000,000
17	21,843,987,843,214,700,000,000
18	168,684,126,344,825,000,000,000
19	1,225,179,458,504,510,000,000,000
20	8,392,478,290,755,940,000,000,000
21	54,351,294,454,419,400,000,000,000
22	333,519,306,879,391,000,000,000,000
23	1,943,112,463,558,190,000,000,000,000
24	10,768,681,679,718,300,000,000,000,000
25	56,855,471,268,912,900,000,000,000,000
26	286,464,105,239,522,000,000,000,000,000
27	1,379,271,617,819,920,000,000,000,000,000
28	6,354,501,382,098,520,000,000,000,000,000
29	28,047,454,376,160,700,000,000,000,000,000
30	116,734,223,525,747,000,000,000,000,000,000
31	462,597,166,588,521,000,000,000,000,000,000
32	1,885,145,181,986,410,000,000,000,000,000,000
33	7,083,575,635,342,880,000,000,000,000,000,000
34	25,825,877,286,681,600,000,000,000,000,000,000
35	89,324,486,542,147,300,000,000,000,000,000,000
36	300,229,524,211,105,000,000,000,000,000,000,000
37	973,717,375,819,804,000,000,000,000,000,000,000
38	3,049,272,834,804,120,000,000,000,000,000,000,000
39	9,226,004,987,356,070,000,000,000,000,000,000,000
40	26,986,064,588,016,400,000,000,000,000,000,000,000
41	76,350,816,883,168,600,000,000,000,000,000,000,000
42	209,055,806,132,485,000,000,000,000,000,000,000,000
43	554,240,979,700,078,000,000,000,000,000,000,000,000
44	1,423,391,606,957,010,000,000,000,000,000,000,000,000
45	3,542,663,585,093,020,000,000,000,000,000,000,000,000
46	8,546,601,167,269,690,000,000,000,000,000,000,000,000
47	20,007,364,480,890,700,000,000,000,000,000,000,000,000
48	45,433,390,175,356,100,000,000,000,000,000,000,000,000
49	100,138,900,794,662,000,000,000,000,000,000,000,000,000
50	214,297,247,700,577,000,000,000,000,000,000,000,000,000
51	445,402,122,671,786,000,000,000,000,000,000,000,000,000
52	899,369,670,779,573,000,000,000,000,000,000,000,000,000
53	1,764,800,863,416,520,000,000,000,000,000,000,000,000,000
54	3,366,194,239,479,660,000,000,000,000,000,000,000,000,000
55	6,242,760,225,944,090,000,000,000,000,000,000,000,000,000
56	11,269,263,978,934,800,000,000,000,000,000,000,000,000,000
57	19,753,094,699,885,700,000,000,000,000,000,000,000,000,000
58	33,716,489,229,115,300,000,000,000,000,000,000,000,000,000
59	56,003,660,075,479,700,000,000,000,000,000,000,000,000,000
60	90,539,250,455,359,000,000,000,000,000,000,000,000,000,000
61	142,486,900,716,630,900,000,000,000,000,000,000,000,000,000
62	218,328,386,194,837,000,000,000,000,000,000,000,000,000,000
63	325,759,817,306,582,000,000,000,000,000,000,000,000,000,000
64	473,369,734,523,627,000,000,000,000,000,000,000,000,000,000
65	670,000,238,633,441,000,000,000,000,000,000,000,000,000,000
66	923,788,209,191,564,000,000,000,000,000,000,000,000,000,000
67	1,240,909,534,734,930,000,000,000,000,000,000,000,000,000,000
68	1,624,131,596,932,480,000,000,000,000,000,000,000,000,000,000
69	2,071,356,239,566,070,000,000,000,000,000,000,000,000,000,000
70	2,574,389,897,746,400,000,000,000,000,000,000,000,000,000,000
71	3,118,287,200,987,190,000,000,000,000,000,000,000,000,000,000
72	3,681,311,277,880,710,000,000,000,000,000,000,000,000,000,000
73	4,236,029,415,643,960,000,000,000,000,000,000,000,000,000,000
74	4,751,222,182,411,020,000,000,000,000,000,000,000,000,000,000
75	5,194,669,586,102,720,000,000,000,000,000,000,000,000,000,000
76	5,536,424,164,135,790,000,000,000,000,000,000,000,000,000,000
77	5,752,129,001,699,520,000,000,000,000,000,000,000,000,000,000
78	5,825,874,245,311,060,000,000,000,000,000,000,000,000,000,000

Fig 12 – Combinations with Reversals

You can see how instead of just doubling, things increase exponentially. Let's use a 5 card set as an example. Out of the standard 78 (e.g. no reversals), that numbers just over 21 million combinations. Impressive enough but consider that when reversals are included we go from over 21 million to over 721 million.

Positional meaning—Each of the 76,076 unique 3 card combinations counted above only need to have an exact set of 3 that is not repeated in any of the other sets. Our unique counts do not account for positions. Mind, Body, Spirit is one kind of 3 card template. Well, you could draw 3 cards for that template, say Hermit, Star and Lover. The Hermit in this case is obviously interpreted as relating to the mind. But you could pull the exact same 3 cards for the exact same template and have them come out Lover, Hermit, Star. That equals an entirely different read even though it is the same 3 card combination in the table above. After all, the Lover is now a mental prompt about the mind and the Hermit has switched to be about the body, etc. To see how the numbers change when accounting for all this we need to leave combinations aside and move on to permutations.

Permutations

Well, we've gone this far so why not display the near infinite ranges provided by our ancient relic when you simply allow for the re-sequencing of cards within a certain combination as described above? We know our Hermit, Star and Lover triumvirate from above gets counted as 1 in our combinations model, period. Calculating permutations however allows Hermit, Star and Lover to be counted separately from Star, Hermit, Lover, etc.

We have to use notated versions of the totals this time

because the numbers themselves are so gargantuan, even compared to the ones above. For a sense of the exponential explosion, just note that the 3 card combination figure was 76,076 but the 3 card permutation total is 456,456. Here is the largest number from the below table but written out fully . . .

11,324,281,178,206,297,831,457,521,158,732,046,228,731,
749,579,488,251,990,048,962,825,668,835,325,234,200,76
6,245,086,213,177,344,000,000,000,000,000,000.

You can see how quickly the below totals obliterate the maximum threshold reached in our combination tables. Unfortunately, the use of notated totals means we lose the elegant shaping of the Totals column. Still you can see that our permutation numbers take things to an even more unimaginable level.

Permutations without Reversals . . .

Number of cards:	Totals:
1	78
2	6,006
3	456,456
4	34,234,200
5	2,533,330,800
6	184,933,148,400
7	13,315,186,684,800
8	945,378,254,620,800
9	66,176,477,823,456,000
10	4.57E+18
11	3.11E+20
12	2.08E+22
13	1.37E+24
14	8.92E+25

Number of cards:	Totals:
15	5.71E+27
16	3.60E+29
17	2.23E+31
18	1.36E+33
19	8.17E+34
20	4.82E+36
21	2.79E+38
22	1.59E+40
23	8.92E+41
24	4.91E+43
25	2.65E+45
26	1.40E+47
27	7.30E+48
28	3.72E+50
29	1.86E+52
30	9.12E+53
31	4.38E+55
32	2.06E+57
33	9.47E+58
34	4.26E+60
35	1.87E+62
36	8.06E+63
37	3.39E+65
38	1.39E+67
39	5.55E+68
40	2.17E+70
41	8.23E+71
42	3.04E+73
43	1.10E+75
44	3.84E+76
45	1.30E+78
46	4.30E+79

Number of cards:	Totals:
47	1.38E+81
48	4.27E+82
49	1.28E+84
50	3.71E+85
51	1.04E+87
52	2.81E+88
53	7.30E+89
54	1.83E+91
55	4.38E+92
56	1.01E+94
57	2.22E+95
58	4.65E+96
59	9.31E+97
60	1.77E+99
61	3.18E+100
62	5.41E+101
63	8.66E+102
64	1.30E+104
65	1.82E+105
66	2.36E+106
67	2.84E+107
68	3.12E+108
69	3.12E+109
70	2.81E+110
71	2.25E+111
72	1.57E+112
73	9.44E+112
74	4.72E+113
75	1.89E+114
76	5.66E+114
77	1.13E+115
78	1.13E+115

Permutations with Reversals . . .

Number of cards:	Totals:
1	156
2	24,180
3	3723720
4	569,729,160
5	86,598,832,320
6	13,076,423,680,320
7	1,961,463,552,048,000
8	292,258,069,255,152,100
9	4.33E+19
10	6.36E+21
11	9.28E+23
12	1.35E+26
13	1.94E+28
14	2.77E+30
15	3.94E+32
16	5.55E+34
17	7.77E+36
18	1.08E+39
19	1.49E+41
20	2.04E+43
21	2.78E+45
22	3.75E+47
23	5.02E+49
24	6.68E+51
25	8.82E+53
26	1.16E+56
27	1.50E+58
28	1.94E+60
29	2.48E+62
30	3.15E+64

Number of cards:	Totals:
31	3.97E+66
32	4.96E+68
33	6.15E+70
34	7.57E+72
35	9.23E+74
36	1.12E+77
37	1.34E+79
38	1.59E+81
39	1.88E+83
40	2.20E+85
41	2.55E+87
42	2.94E+89
43	3.35E+91
44	3.78E+93
45	4.24E+95
46	4.70E+97
47	5.17E+99
48	5.64E+101
49	6.09E+103
50	6.52E+105
51	6.91E+107
52	7.25E+109
53	7.54E+111
54	7.77E+113
55	7.93E+115
56	8.01E+117
57	8.01E+119
58	7.93E+121
59	7.77E+123
60	7.53E+125
61	7.23E+127
62	6.87E+129

Number of cards:	Totals:
63	6.46E+131
64	6.01E+133
65	5.53E+135
66	5.03E+137
67	4.53E+139
68	4.03E+141
69	3.54E+143
70	3.08E+145
71	2.65E+147
72	2.25E+149
73	1.89E+151
74	1.57E+153
75	1.29E+155
76	1.04E+157
77	8.35E+158
78	6.60E+160

The numbers of permutations jump so quickly that we only make it to 6 card spreads before reaching hundreds of billions (without reversals). This is astonishing and the figures are really too much to comprehend. Due to this there aren't as many individual points of interests or analogies to pull out from the permutations as there were from the combinations. After all, how do you go bigger as a comparison point than all of the stars in all of the galaxies in existence? Regardless, understanding the real extent of the universe(s) contained within the Tarot is a worthy exercise.

*   *   *

Can we actually increase the numbers even further? Yes, but we won't. We accounted for changing card positions within a template but not for different templates. Put simply, the

Hermit, Star, Lover trio in a Past, Present, Future spread could be counted as different when seen in a Mind, Body, Spirit spread. Another X factor is the variety of Tarot decks available. Cards rendered by one artist can be noticeably different from the depiction in a traditional Marseille or Rider-Waite-Smith one. Do we then count those as different sets even over and above what was computed in our tables? Well we could but we don't need to go that far. For one thing no one has any idea how many variant Tarot decks exist. Just know that this makes for one more possible multiplier. We won't take on the different template factor for similar reasons. Just know that the numbers could expand even further.

These then are the underlying depths hidden in our house of worship and introspection talisman. If casting the cards creates a manageable version of the whole, the reader and querent are still actually connecting to a practically if not literally limitless master plan. If that plan was completely built out, the mansion would be galactic in size. Imagine door after door, room after room, continuing on in an expansive network.

Now what if we were to put practical dimensions on those features (rooms) and then extrapolate a literal size for our castle based on the numbers in our tables? At this point it would be a shame not to. If each individual space was the size of a typical living room, and all of these rooms were connected together on one floor, the resulting square shaped building would be about *272 times larger than the Milky Way Galaxy.* Remember earlier in this chapter when I said you'd imagine more doors than you ever have before?

That model involves using every possible spread within the Tarot but what if we bring things closer to the reality of how people have historically drawn the cards? If we only counts spreads from 1 to 12 cards, then our much humbler building would still be twice as long as our solar system. And that is keeping things as small as possible (combinations with no reversals) so let's look at the bookend to that. 1 to 12 card spreads in terms of permutations with reversals would require well over 1 million galaxies the size of ours to match the resulting building.

We can't memorize the colossal numbers reviewed in our tables but the appreciation can remain. Speaking of exploring these spaces, it is actually possible to imagine stepping through some of the smallest categories. The 3,003 combinations and 6,006 permutations available from 2 card draws are a good example. I don't know how long it would take to walk through either of those sets of rooms but our minds can actually comprehend accomplishing it. Adding just one card seemingly moves us beyond the realm of the possible though. After all, walking through either 76,076 or 456,456 rooms feels Sisyphus-like in scope.

Things quickly move to the all but unimaginable from there. So, a new mental exercise can now be added to our previous visualization. That one was based on an individual spread and its few cards. This one consists of simply imagining walking through our labyrinth where each room is a specific spread from the innumerable possibilities quantified in this chapter. It's an impossible task but just see how far you can get even if each room is just a vague image in your mind. It likely won't be very far at first. Many people use journals to write their thoughts about the cards and mature as readers. Writing a description or even drawing an impression of the rooms or halls encountered can be a progressive task. How large would that narrative or picture collection be after a year of expanding it based on just one kind of spread, say 2 card sets?

Going with our overall logic regarding visualization as an

additional way to explore the Tarot, why not have a particular method for internalizing and imagining the actual vastness of it? Historian and Pulitzer Prize winner John Meacham said that cathedrals were designed to awe us, to make us feel small. This one assuredly does.

CHAPTER 7

EXPLORING AN IMAGINARY ARCHEOLOGY

"We shape our buildings; thereafter they shape us."
Winston Churchill[34]

THE VISUALIZATION EXERCISES proposed in this book are meant to provide a practical benefit. Doing actual reads is not the only way to increase your skill with the cards. Think of it like professional athletes whose practices are composed of much more than actually competing or scrimmaging. They spend much of their time performing individual drills that focus on the development of a particular skill. There are of course existing exercises, many of which are beneficial but we are here to add to the existing lore and in a new way.

To quickly recap, we've already elucidated 3 different methods so far. Let's walk through them in a new order and then add another.

Method 1 – Imagine it all

Imagine the concepts and complexities contained within the Tarot as a physical structure. What does it look like? Trying to design it forces you to think over the many overlapping aspects at play. As an example we could envision a 3 leveled ziggurat. The bottom, widest layer represents the pips. The middle layer is narrower and is the court cards. The slimmest and highest is the major arcana. How many sides does the bottom level have? This time let's say 78, each with its own door. After all, each card is an entryway into the Tarot. Once you enter any one of them, imagine a forest of giant pillars supporting the structure above. We can imagine 40 of them since there are that many pip cards and they could be divided into 4 sections, 1 for each suit just as the cards are. However, a more sophisticated vision would be to have 4 sets of 55 columns each. Confused? Each pip series is numbered 1 to 10 (e.g. Ace of Coins, 2 of Coins, 3 of Coins, etc.). $1+2+3+4+5+6+7+8+9+10$ $= 55$. And with 4 suits that gives us 220 total columns. At this particular time I prefer to think of it that way, so every suit-section has 10 groupings of pillars. The 3 of Batons card would then be a 3 column grouping slightly separated from the rest. Each section has 1 column that stands alone, the Ace, and these are wider than the others and feature elaborate decoration.

Above this tremendous space is the 2nd level for the courts. It's divided into 4, each subsection directly above its minor pips. Each of those 4 sections is divided into smaller sections as well. Let's picture the characters here as statues high up on the walls of that unreachable but visible 2nd level. The kings, queens, knights and pages sit within a vertical hierarchy. The royal couple are side by side, below them is their knight and below him is his page.

Finally the smallest of the levels looks down onto the floor from even higher. It is 22 sided and in this example we'll say there are massive stained glass windows representing each of the trumps. They form a circle, looking together down into the center of the ground floor.

Now picture standing on the first floor somewhere and trying to take in what you can see. You can't focus on 258 objects at once (220+16+22). Just like standing outside of Notre Dame, you have to choose where to look. Your location might dictate a line of sight that encompasses a few of the column groupings from different suits. Peeking down from an exposed angle is a court card or two and above them the light of 1 atout window shines directly onto the nexus of everything you're seeing. Everything else is relegated to your peripheral vision and obscured by tricks of shadow and angle. That is a spread, that is focusing on just the aspects a given set of cards tells you to, which is actually not what we're doing with this exercise but you can see the natural flow. Everything we just covered is one of countless ways to create the overarching, all-encompassing Tarot structure in our minds.

And that was a very simple example as we know, recalling the thematic linkages between the digits (a series of 10 separate 1's versus 2's, etc.) and so much more. How surprising is it that the 258 individual elements can combine in various ways into the astronomical figures we now know exist?

A more ambitious version of imagining it all could go in any number of directions. Just trying to layer in the shallowest level of visual motifs from a given deck is a challenge that greatly complicates the above. But doing so is fun and, I think, productive. I love the colors in the traditional Marseille Tarot deck and use them when reading. Accounting for that when visually imagining it all in any kind of meaningful way is no mean feat. However, just trying to will force you to think about the colors and how they're distributed throughout the cards on a deeper level than you ever have before.

So that is the first exercise, what can you create that captures it all, whatever that ends up meaning to you? It can be anything, there is no wrong answer. All that matters is if the imagined structure helps you think more profoundly about the Tarot's real one.

Method 2 – Room by Room

Pull 1 to 3 cards at most, lay them down, *quickly* draw a coherent message out of what you see and move on to the next spread. Do the same and continue the process. As we know, just 2 cards provide thousands of possible hands to work through and 3 explodes into the hundreds of thousands. Also, a larger hand by its nature can't be quickly encapsulated. The ancient Greek philosopher Heraclitus famously said that you can never step into the same river twice.[35] Similarly even a 2 card spread that you've seen before is never read the exact same way. And finally, the point is not to get good at regurgitating off the shelf definitions of individual cards or specific combinations but to create your own.

Running through a gamut of 2 card draws is an excellent way to force yourself to account for card relationships while keeping things simple. A common mistake for beginners is that they have barely established a hold on the individual cards themselves but are trying to follow a popular 10 card template or whatnot with all of it's assorted (and arbitrary) positional meanings on top of trying to keep the symbolism of each card in mind. This exercise allows you to establish a stronger mastery over the cards and how they relate to each other by keeping the numbers and combinations low.

But how do we do this visually? Well, by going room by

room. Every time you throw down 1, 2, or 3 cards, picture
you've walked into 1 room of our never ending mansion. The
Knight of Coins and the 2 or Batons for instance . . . a stone
room with two trees growing in the center, on the opposite
wall is a suit of armor with a coin emblazoned on its chest. As
discussed, batons or rods often represent passion and the fire
element so they (the trees) are ablaze yet unharmed, like the
biblical burning bush. The armor shines brilliantly in the glare.
We're done; walk past that room and into the next where you
create an entirely different scene based on the next set of cards
you pull. Don't stop, keep going. Even a few minutes spent
doing this will force you to imagine a plethora of vivid imagery.
When you're doing so, imagine the galactic-sized labyrinth that
you're working your way through.

Keeping in mind the enormity of the numbers from our
earlier chapter when doing so can give a sense of scale to what
you're doing. If you go through a dozen 2 card rooms, you've
worked your way through just .002 of the total that exist.

Method 3 - Each Spread Builds a Temple

We touched on this way of practice with the druidic-like spread
from an earlier chapter. This is obviously similar to the previous
exercise but here we take it slower and try to use all the nuance
in a given spread. It would also tend to be done with a larger
number of cards. We're also not confined to a simple room or
repeatable structure. The imagination muscles get to work a
little harder here. That's how we ended with a quasi-outdoor
space inside of a larger one. I mean, why not?

Picture a 4 card hand and think of all the interlocking
factors you'd want to account for in your design. Let's imagine
the following cards, Ace of Cups, Page of Batons, Tower, 2 of
Coins. That's quite a bit to take in. We have 3 suits, a person

and a force (major arcana card) to meld into . . . something. How to make it all fit? The Tower is a large structure. Are we going to include it in actual size? Let's do that and put ourselves inside of it. For those experienced at reading, have you ever once imagined yourself inside of the Tower? The answer to that question is usually no. This is the deeper connection that exercises like these can help us form. We're inside the Tower, lightning is striking the roof, sparks and flames are bursting through the ceiling and rain is pouring down the hole that's been made. At the center of the ground floor is a large beautiful vessel, the Ace of Cups. It collects some of the rainwater that is coming down. Inside of it and at its base you see two shining gold coins, like pennies that were thrown into a fountain. The Page is there with his baton in hand. What does he do? Maybe he's barring the door with his two handed baton, trying to keep more of the chaos outside from finding its way in.

Well, that's one way to combine those elements. What is interesting is that the way you choose to visualize it says a lot about you at the time you try, just like reading the cards in the standard way does. I initially read the spread as the following . . . *When trying to keep chaos and confusion from inhibiting your work or project you need to accept some of it as part of the process.* I'm personally feeling pretty challenged with work at the moment so my scene unconsciously played into that. If I was in a different place in life I might have imagined the Tower off in the distance, the rumble of thunder and flash of lightning barely discernible.

And that is not the extent of the layering that can take place. There were 2 coins and 2 is the number of the Papesse or High Priestess. The Tower in most people's minds and representations nowadays is not a religious structure but older decks called it the House of God (and/or Hospital, incidentally). Putting those 2 things together adds a stronger spiritual tint to the spread and so the architecture of the Tower in this version is explicitly religious. If that is the case then the water collecting in the Ace of Cups is holy water in a way and the coins shimmering at the bottom are thereby consecrated. This overall depiction then modifies the meaning to be about a project or effort that has a higher calling than pedestrian career struggles. So, I found the message to be about my creative endeavors, this book being one example. 2 is not a large number, not even in the 1 to 10 range that the pip cards exist in. The money (back to coins) I make from my passion projects is, sadly, infinitesimal compared to my actual career earnings. Regardless, the point is that this reinforces the refined interpretation and encourages me to remember I do not write books, etc. because of whatever monetary reward may result. 2 is also a number of growth, things are starting out and still increasing so there is the prospect of material compensation increasing if I stay focused on the real reason I write, etc. Lastly, if you go way back to Chapter 2 you will see that the baton suit can represent work as well. That seems quite appropriate here given what the reading, both versions of it, made me think through.

The Tower scene in my mind is far more vivid than the description I could write out here. It is part of what all of the methods proposed in this book help with, separating yourself even further from the distractions of the mundane when reading the cards. The further you step into the castle, etc. the richer the experience will be and presumably the more fruitful the result.

Method 4 - Pen to Paper

I should call this method, "Something you might be able to do but I can't (well)." Graphic artists have long been attracted to and inspired by the cards. The rich tradition of reinventing the images on the cards accounts for the great majority of visual exploration of the Tarot that takes place today. It's not the only way as there is Tarot inspired art made in the world that is not restricted to actual Tarot cards.

Our 4th method would be a part of the latter, should anyone with the requisite skills care to try it. The idea is that if you do imagine any of the things from the previous 3 methods, literally draw or paint them. The giant 3 part ziggurat I mentally envisioned earlier looks amazing outside and in, but you'll just have to trust me on that because I'm incapable of rendering it on paper. And we don't have to belabor the suggestion of this 4th method as the concept, if not the execution, is simple. If you have the skills, try painting or drawing any of the scenes that come to mind when performing any of the previous exercises.

Unlike so many traditions where you receive a vision, or hope to, the agency here is entirely with the practitioner. You will the vision into being. And then, you are free to capture it if so inclined. The novelty is that the artist is encouraged to neither stay restricted within the individual card templates nor operate completely in the abstract. The scenes captured would be based on the structures and features of the deck or a particular spread. And as we well know, even a million, heck 10 million, paintings would capture just the tiniest fraction of the total dioramas available.

It must be admitted that this method's inclusion comes from a fairly selfish place in that I would just love to see talented artists bring particular spreads to life much less try to visually capture the grandeur of the entire Tarot. In all seriousness it does seem a natural extension of the visual re-imagination that has been going on for generations.

The writer David Warburton said, "Monumental religious architecture preceded verbal meaning in religion by millennia."[36] Continuing this prehistoric visual dialogue with a man-made sacred place/thing is a central part of what makes the Tarot a vibrant experience. And that's why using new visualization methods to read the Tarot is a natural progression of the art, and one that connects with its heart.

CHAPTER 8

BUILDING BLOCKS

"By their very nature, their testimony is never spontaneous, it is always reticent, fluid, ambiguous, if not fallacious... The most beautiful perfectly preserved statue may perhaps tell us whence the diorite came from which it was quarried, allowing us to induce some kind of commerce with the owners of the deposit, but by itself it cannot ever answer the question of questions: What is it? And why this image?" Assyriologist Bottero[37]

MANY ANCIENT PLACES of worship were built of pieces that had to be acquired, transported to the holy site and shaped for their various purposes (walls, columns, etc.). The Temple of Solomon used materials that came from Mount Lebanon including its famed cedar trees. That mountain was part of an entirely different kingdom and a site 500 kilometers away via today's modern highways. The Pantheon, which we'll discuss below, features massive pillars that were made from granite monoliths quarried out of the ground in Egypt and brought all the way to Rome, then fashioned into shape. Baalbek, Lebanon is site to a temple of Jupiter built by the Romans. What is remarkable about it is that it was built on the foundation of an unfinished earlier and mysterious Phoenician temple. That work in progress had a distinctive Phoenician trait, giant foundation stones. There are 3 of them and each weighs 1,000 tons. For comparison, a Stonehenge monolith weighs 1/40th of that. It was the Scottish traveler David Urquhart who in 1860 brought the mystery of these stones to light. As the *New Yorker* asked, "What . . . was the point of cutting such enormous rocks? And why do it out there in the middle of nowhere, instead of in a capital or a port? Why were there no other sites that looked like Baalbek?"[38]

Forgive the extra archeological details but hopefully these real life examples show how much effort went into building one of these places. Plus, foundational slabs that weigh roughly 2 million pounds each might be a good way to picture a foundation strong enough for the structures imagined earlier.

The type of Herculean efforts just detailed, even metaphorically, are not necessary for us as the pieces for our building are ready to use in the form of the cards. They have also been transported but that is something we can measure in time as well as distance. The original work of digging out the stones and cutting down the trees was done centuries ago. Meanwhile, on the one hand we can say the process of fashioning was completed a long time ago if using a historical deck but it's also still being done by artists today. Even the artist designing a new deck as we speak is using those ancient materials, and that is how the Tarot stays rooted while still evolving.

We previously gave a brief overview of how the cards are divided into their constituent categories and have dealt at length with how the pieces can create a dizzying number of combinations. Let's now focus on the pieces themselves. Just as with our deck overview we will be fairly brief.

The Major Arcana- These are obviously the most important

cards in the deck. They therefore speak the loudest. To quickly reiterate a point, only they received individual artistic attention when the Tarot was invented and for most of its use. They are the heart of the archetypal iconography that gives the Tarot so much symbolic potency. These are the features of our house of worship that cannot be ignored. If you walk into St. Peter's Basilica in Rome, you will be inundated with imagery in the cavernous space. Consequently there are many things you can miss but others you can't such as the enormous central altar. The major arcana cannot be missed in our overall building regardless of what form they take. They are statues that loom large over everything else, giant stained glass windows whose images shine down as in our ziggurat example, 22 towers that give shape to the inner and outer castle, etc. And still they're part of a complicated whole.

Fig 13 - The Pantheon drawn inside and out.

The original Pantheon, coincidentally also in Rome, would be a good example of what we mean. One of the masterpieces of ancient architecture, it celebrated a multitude of gods as its name implies.

"This is the most perfect of all the remains of antiquity. Formerly the temple of all the gods, it has since been dedicated to all the saints; and the great and invisible spirit, the source of all things, is perhaps in the contemplation of the modern, as of the ancient worshipers of the Pantheon."[39]

The Pantheon's perfection comes from its lack of uniformity. The front is angular, a triangle on top of a rectangle. The rear is a cylinder capped by a dome. The hybrid architecture is to this day its calling card and has amazed people for thousands of years. Originally there were statues of many gods being honored by this building lining the interior. They were the major arcana of this temple. We're on to something with our Tarot concept-building after all it would seem.

"But we linger too long at the threshold; let us pass through its open gates of ancient bronze, and enter the temple. How beautiful the proportions, how perfect the symmetry, how noble the design! The eye takes in at once the whole majesty of its magic circle, glances over the lofty columns of ancient marble that divide its parts, and, rising from the variegated pavement on which we tread, rests on that swelling dome whose top is open to the clear blue sky, and through which the light seems to descend uninterrupted in its purest ray from heaven." *Rome, In the Nineteenth Century*, Vol 1 1817[40]

The Pantheon makes a remarkable example of our concept brought to life but back to the major arcana. They retain an air of mystery no matter how much has been written about them and this is something they should keep. It is a mistake to try and pin them down too specifically. The ancient oracles gave somewhat ambiguous answers to the questions posed to them. We can't pin down the meaning of the look on the faces in much ancient art, sacred and secular. A Christian cannot precisely explain the nature of the Holy Trinity. And the original worshippers in the Pantheon surely stared up at the statues of their gods and found them largely unknowable.

The major arcana should likewise not be reduced to a rule based matrix where each is captured in an index card like definition. Those massive images have to remain somewhat impenetrable to the visitor looking up at their impassive masks.

Remember that according to Jung the archetypes go back to prehistory. Their true origin is lost to us. Likewise, who's to say what certain images and patterns meant to the evolving human mind? It can even be difficult to say what these symbols mean to us now and we have the added complexity of using a set of symbols captured centuries back by people who would have made different associations than either their ancestors or descendants.

Just for the record, I am not arguing against understanding the historical context of the original images as much as possible. That was actually the Tarot book I had started on when this project came to mind and then took over.

Anyway, back to our church tour; know that whatever physical features these 22 cards take, they are the ones that speak most deeply to the viewer. That is also how they should play into a reading.

The Suits & Minor Arcana- As we know, all of the remaining 56 cards are divided into the 4 suits. The mysterious, more divine trumps are free from such classifications, buttressing our point from above. We don't map out heaven. But we do break things down into categories here on Earth and 4 is a common way to do it. We innately orient everything around us by front, behind, left and right. There are 4 cardinal directions and the year is divided into 4 seasons. So it's appropriate that all the cards below the trumps are divided up into the suits because now we've moved from the heavenly level to the Earth bound but still elevated realm, the courts.

Royalty and their attendants lived in castles, separated from the existence of the commoners. Our 16 royals and servants share the suits but are likewise apart from the rest of the minor arcana just as the king of Bohemia was specifically the king of Bohemia's residents yet really lived apart from them. Nor did he rule over another king's realm as the King of Cups has no suzerainty over the baton cards.

In fact historical royalty expressly embraced this nature as the middle ground between the heavenly and mortal reaches. They ruled as agents of the upper dwelling deities or as Earth dwelling gods themselves. A global manifestation of this belief was the tradition noted in *The Golden Bough* wherein it was considered sacrilegious for a priestly king to touch the ground with his feet. Many societies went to outrageous lengths to prevent this from happening.[41]

There are also different levels at play as the king and queen rule over the knight, with the page serving beneath all of them. So if these court cards are represented on their own level, there is still a hierarchical distinction among them to be somehow represented. This is just another indication of how the Tarot system if imagined visually is multi-dimensional.

And no matter how many scales or divisions you think

of, you can always think of more. Imagine the lowest layer containing just the aces, the next the 1's, the next the 2's, etc. After the 10's you'd reach the level of the pages, then up and up until the circle of the major arcana reigned above them all.

That would equal 15 levels. You'll notice we went for a simpler 3 level design earlier. You really can just keep redesigning the blueprints if you will. It is an endless but productive process that keeps reminding the practitioner of the depth the deck contains. Back to our nobility, these pieces are the bridge between the upper and lower levels. It's important to note that they are the only level that shares characteristics with the other 2. They have characteristics of the atouts with their visual personifications and archetypal images but are also suit bound like the minor pips.

So many real world temples literally reach for the sky with their upper portions yet have their worshippers stay on the ground. The court cards are like the arches in those buildings that connect the columns from below with the domes and spires from above.

And lastly of course we come the minor pips. The divisions of the Pantheon again form a useful guide. The portico at the front of the building is crammed with multiple rows of giant pillars, each weighing 50 metric tons by the way. They hint of the pips which support the rest of the Tarot. They are not as symbolically potent as the two tiers above them but are indispensable nonetheless. We may instinctively look towards the top of the pyramids at Giza but the more numerous stone blocks are those of the wider, lower levels.

In a way the minor pips are the most complicated pieces of all when illustrated in the traditional manner because a looming central character gives our minds something to grab on to and we don't get that here. Via the Jungian process outlined previously, this gets our minds moving as we are visual and storytelling creatures. The Rider-Waite-Smith deck likely resulted in the great expansion of Tarot for this reason; there was now more for the viewer to easily (e.g. visually) grasp. So in the traditional version of the pips, reading has to be done in a more challenging manner. I should say manners because, unsurprisingly, there is more than one way to do this.

The various pieces that make up our building materials can be well understood in terms of how they fit together, but will never be fully understood in terms of what they are. Recall this chapter's opening quotation from an expert in Assyrian archeology. Looking at a statue from one of the world's oldest civilizations he knew he would never really grasp the 'why.' It is the same with our ancient artifact. Why a hermit and not some other equally potent character/symbol in one of the coveted 22 spots? What exactly should we read from his facial expression? How did someone decide to wed the trumps to standard playing cards? We will never know the answers to these questions and countless others. And yet, we have a systematic, fairly easy to use (but not master) way to assemble our pieces and make something special, something like a modern Pantheon.

CHAPTER 9

SAINTS, MONSTERS AND CASTLES

"There are no rules of architecture for a castle in the clouds." Gilbert K. Chesterton[42]

O UR *THE HUNCHBACK of Notre Dame* quotation earlier noted the collection of beings Quasimodo could commune with inside of and outside of his cathedral. Our artifact of course has its own assortment. The difference is Quasimodo's experience was purely intuitive. He had no text book telling him that he should think of a particular emotion or whatnot when gazing at a particular statue. Seeing a specific gargoyle did not mean that supposedly scenario X or Y was about to play out in his life.

Enter the various, existing and often contradictory teachings on the Tarot. What to make of it all when the authorities can't agree, even monumentally influential ones from the same time and movement like Waite and Crowley? A common question from a beginner trying to interpret a spread involves how they've gone to different websites and come away more confused than they were when they started. Maybe it would be better if our castle in the clouds truly had no rules as Victorian writer, poet, philosopher and more Gilbert K. Chesterton might have suggested. As discussed, the shift from game cards to divination tool was gradual and only became formalized in late modernity. And as we know, the pre-existing literature about the cards as an esoteric tool was invented material. It's not then surprising that dueling methods and contradictory advice ended up existing side by side.

* * *

Reading is often divided into two broad categories within the Tarot community . . . logical and intuitive. A purely logical read would involve following given rules/definitions of whichever methodology you're using to an exacting degree. Each card has preset definitions, the same is true for their reversed forms. The spread you use will define what each card represents based on its position in the chosen template. Shuffle the cards as directed (or they won't work!), and on and on. The problem here is easy for even a complete novice to see. It is very pedantic but more importantly the visual-archetypal-unconscious mind experience is missing.

Conversely though a purely intuitive read would involve no guidance of any kind, just gazing at the images in the abstract and seeing what revelations or messages come. This approach is equally problematic. Despite disagreements, there is often a broad consensus on overall card meanings and there is collected wisdom in that. Ignoring that body of knowledge means missing valuable clues as to how best absorb a certain image.

Luckily no one actually reads in a 100% logical or intuitive way. Well probably not, but the point is the danger is in skewing too strongly to either side. Preference is not a problem, everyone leans more heavily on one over the other. But each reader should strive for a healthy balance. Doing so avoids the dueling extremes of being too . . .

- Shackled (Logical)—The 10 of Swords by definition means betrayal, loss or hardship. That is a definition that was invented in modernity and based on an image assigned to the card in the 20th century. More critically, it is overly specific and therefore limiting.

- Unmoored (Intuitive)—The images have no generally accepted, historically grounded understanding. Cups can mean one thing today but swords can mean that same thing tomorrow. If symbols have no consistency in interpretation then they have no connection to history, prehistory or psychology.

The approach recommended in this work is not just to find balance or to find the right balance for you as that's rather obvious if still important. The recommendation is to keep refining until you have a deeply personal method. I intensely love history so that comes out in my readings. I prefer the older version of the cards and the simpler minor pips, I try to use what we know about late medieval/early Renaissance mindsets and symbolism to draw meaning from the cards. The commonly held, high level interpretations of the cards matter to me as well as they are part of the history of the Tarot's development. I may be overly fond of reminding people that the great majority of the teachings taken so seriously today were recently invented (historically speaking) but generations have worked on that body of knowledge. It is a tradition of its own at this point and one going strong after more than a century. Still, it's of far lower importance for me than the historical context.

All of that is on the logical side but if you care to go back to my Tower scene-reading, you'll see that I freely intuit based on the images of the cards. So I personally put a premium on the historical circumstances of the cards' original development, take the modern lore under advisement and then allow myself to freely associate based on the images I see. I am to be clear not recommending that approach to anyone. Unlike many books on this subject, the point is not to instruct the reader on how to read the cards but to just to instruct him or her to understand the opposing approaches and eventually (for the novice) develop a way of reading that uses both sides of the coin, literally both sides of your brain, and works as a form of personal expression. In short, don't ignore the rules and don't be enslaved by them as you build your own castle in the clouds.

CHAPTER 10

SYMBOLS AS STATUES, STATUES AS SYMBOLS

"What Jung felt was that symbols were those elements . . . that compelled our attention and directed our energies toward . . . the ineffable." John Van Eenwyk, Ph.D. in religion and psychology[43]

W<small>E'VE CONSIDERED ALL</small> 78 cards in their various groupings but especially in their 3 tiers. The final step is to look in depth at the individual pieces of art that dominate whatever temple we build, at least when they're present . . . the trumps. They are each a symbol that points us to the ineffable and the ineffable is that which is, "Too great or extreme to be expressed or described in words."[44]

The admonition against trying to define the Tarot's symbols too specifically is well taken. It is also what we said in regard to the major arcana specifically but all the cards generally. Despite that we will do as practically every Tarot book before has done and tour the 22 cards that made the Tarot what it is.

A brief note on 2 of the sub-headings for each card. *Consensus* is a distillation of the most commonly encountered

Tarot teachings and *Additional interpretation* attempts to add something new or highlight something overlooked.

Also, I will use the classic Marseille Tarot as the baseline version of the cards but this is not just a tour of one deck's specific visuals. Instead we'll touch on original, old and new when appropriate, really talking about the atouts in their universal aspects. The numbering and sequence are however based on the Marseille since those have to be based on one particular take. Readers who have only ever used some postmodern decks may even be surprised by seeing how the Roman numerals are written. The Hermit (9) is VIIII instead of IX for instance. Lastly, the names on the card images are in French.

The Fool

Fig 14

Consensus—A wandering jester travels free of obligation or expectation. Common ascriptions include freedom, limitlessness, spontaneity, adventure, recklessness.

Background—The court jester, buffoon, clown and tramp can all be seen as part of an archetype that exists from ancient times to the postmodern age. All of them are free of the conventional constraints that govern the rest of society.

This was mirrored by his role in Tarot card games where he allowed the player possessing him to break the rules, sometimes being called the Excuse card for that reason.[45] The modern descendant of that is the contemporary card phrase and playing convention, "Joker's wild."

Additional interpretation—The Fool's freedom comes partly from his being considered harmless. There is a decidedly pitiable aspect to him in his early Tarot representations that was shed in modernity. He was even called the Beggar or Madman early on.[46] In one of his very earliest surviving cards, children amuse themselves by hurling stones at him.[47] In his classic but not earliest depiction he carries a bindle (sack on a stick) with his meager possessions just like the prevalent caricatures of a 20th century hobo or tramp. All in all he was visualized as a bedraggled, mentally ill vagabond in his early incarnations.

But he is also usually depicted as an entertainer who has the freedom to break societal taboos with his pranks and jests. Real life fools could mock whomever they liked and even make overt-comical sexual advances on women during their street performances.

Characters like this frequently led folkloric processions during ritualistic celebrations in Europe that had pagan roots. This survived into the carnival/religious parades that were a common part of Renaissance life. These *triumphal processions* were possibly, perhaps even probably, an important inspiration for the design of the major arcana.[48] As such it is fitting that the Fool normally leads off the pageant of 22 cards.

The Fool is overly romanticized by many because we want

the freedom he has without stopping to think about the steep cost he pays for it.

Miscellaneous—This is usually the only major arcana card with no number, so he can be thought of as being even free of the limits that rule the gods of the deck if you will. Really this was just a practical result of his unique role in the original card game(s). All of the atouts were originally unnumbered, only the Fool managed to preserve this quality.

The Magician, I

Fig 15

Consensus—A magician harnesses cosmic energy to conjure as well as entertain. Common ascriptions include creative energy, transformational power, beginnings, deceit (magic tricks are called tricks for a reason).

Background—Magicians have existed throughout the history of human storytelling under many guises. That this template goes deep into our psyche is exhibited by the fact that even modern historical figures used its attractive power to gain followers and/ or fans. Rasputin and Harry Houdini are two such examples.

It is important to note that there are non-Tarot medieval/ Renaissance images portraying what we think of as the Fool and Magician as the same character.[49] This often overlooked fact helps us understand their pairing and meanings.

Additional interpretation—There is a central mystery to this card that is more pivotal to understanding it than the common emphasis on creative energy. Is this figure capable of harnessing the universe's energy and creating things or is he only adept at convincing you he can through illusion? He is usually drawn as in the prime of life instead of as a wizened figure. This is partly because that other archaic, Merlin-like pattern is handled elsewhere in the major arcana.

This card tells us there is an equally potent pattern in the collective unconscious of a younger, vibrant, magical performer with an emphasis on the word performer. There is always a fresh magician-illusionist (David Blaine and Criss Angel in recent decades) who fills this role in popular culture the way Houdini and others once did. And if you know your history of magic performers, you'll know there's a long association between that and pickpocketing or grifting, precisely as there was with this card's character. But fear not, this doesn't take the magic out of the card (pun intended). We are still captivated by magicians and feel a sense of wonder at how they can seemingly make something appear from nothing. Emulating an act of true creation has in fact been a primal ritual in countless human belief systems.

From a reading perspective, the Magician could be used as

a prompt to consider possible deceit or distraction in the life of the postulant. This can be done instead of or at least in addition to the much more recent master of elements, creative force interpretation encountered today.

Miscellaneous—The above musings about the Magician's authentic aspects are strongly reinforced in a few ways. He was originally portrayed as a humble street performer, a common street-side hustler in fact. In French he is Le Bateleur which translates in part as *charlatan*. He was sometimes depicted with balls and cups which relate to a rigged shell game the likes of which is still used today by sidewalk grifters. Additionally he was also called the Juggler, hardly a man of a mystical bent. These are all clear indications of his original nature as is his shared lineage with the Fool.

The High Priestess, II

Fig 16

Consensus—A high priestess has collected a vast accumulation of knowledge. Common ascriptions include wisdom, sacred knowledge, female intuition.

Background—A priest or priestess teaches us how to understand divinity. Meanwhile goddesses are obviously prevalent throughout the history of mythology. They could be linked to wisdom in opposition to male gods who tended to have more of an action-will orientation. Hence Athena was the goddess of wisdom in ancient Greece as Minerva was in Rome. Seshat was an Egyptian goddess of wisdom and writing, having invented the latter.[50] That is an interesting parallel to the High Priestess who is the only figure of the Tarot traditionally depicted with a book.

Additional interpretation—The dominance of patriarchal societies in early human history resulted in all of the world's largest religions eventually having only priests (e.g. male). The formerly powerful mother-goddess template and the role of priestesses and female shamans was thereby diminished but not extinguished. It may be reflected here, in a product of 15th century Europe no less. I would argue that is even though the Catholic Church was sometimes portrayed as a woman in religious art of the time, including at the Vatican itself, inside of St. Peter's Basilica.[51]

Either way we can think of this card as hinting at neglected or overlooked knowledge/spirituality.

Miscellaneous—The French name for this card is La Pappese (The Popess) and we cannot leave out that this card is a possible a reference to either a mythical or historic female pope, at least of sorts. Legend says that a mid-9th century female Pope of the Catholic Church was expunged from official records in later years. Pope Joan, as the mythical figure is remembered, is portrayed in art of the time although usually pregnant and/or giving birth. This is because the tale states that Joan was found out when she inadvertently gave birth to a child in public.

Meanwhile author Gertrude Moakley first proposed that it was an actual, historic woman named Sister Manfreda who was portrayed on the card. She was declared Pope by a loyal sect, leading to her execution by church inquisitors in 1300. She was also related to the Visconti family of the historic Visconti-Sforza Tarot.[52]

The Empress, III

Fig 17

Consensus—An Empress sits majestically on her throne. Common ascriptions include mother-goddess, Earth-mother, feminine power, maternal nourishing and protection.

Background—Like all of the personages in the major arcana, the Empress can be seen as earthly and divine. All of the focus tends to go to her mythological aspect. She is Gaia, Juno, Hera, Astarte, Isis, Tanit, etc. This taps into the ultimate baseline human experience, being created and shaped by one's mother.

Additional interpretation—Now to the overlooked side. The Cambridge Dictionary says an empress is, "A female ruler of an empire, or the wife of a male ruler of an empire."[53] In the first half of that definition we have a woman ruling in a very direct way, unlike a distant god(ess). So this template is also Queen Elizabeth, Queen Victoria, Catherine the Great, Cleopatra and Tzu Hsi. An in-charge empress or emperor symbolized order to their realms. They established it through active rule and by defending their people from external threats. So this card can also represent the ordering of things in life through a feminine perspective.

Miscellaneous—We mentioned some queens above. Do not let their titles confuse you as Queen Victoria for instance ruled over an empire upon which the Sun never set. The Empress therefore has the discussed earthly-divine duality but an additional one as well. Is she a woman and/or female energy *in charge* or does she rule with a male counterpart in which case she is half of the equation?

The Emperor, IIII

Fig 18

Consensus—An Emperor sits regally on his throne. Common ascriptions include authority, paternal energy, father, god, stability, control, discipline.

Background—We don't even have to bother listing mythical male rulers or historic emperors. The stability, protection and order provided by the sovereign is as present here as with our Empress but from a masculine orientation. And again this can be taken as a very temporal thing, emperors and empresses ruled earthly kingdoms. In fact the earthly ruler aspect was almost certainly what was intended by the card's mysterious creator(s) as we'll see in later chapters.

Additional interpretation—An emperor would not be the most immediate sovereign most people would have in their lives. A king might rule close to home in the emperor's name. The

Emperor and Empress can therefore represent thought, will and control at a global (e.g. higher) level.

Miscellaneous—Does the Emperor rule with the Empress? The Tarot speaks in male vs. female figures but they should not be thought of as literally men and women when reading. Each man and woman has both aspects within themselves. You could say these two cards together represent the perfect ruler because of the inherent balance.

The Pope (Hierophant, High Priest), V

Fig 19

Consensus—A high priest, originally the Pope, officiates or carries out his duties. Common ascriptions include spiritual father, religious teacher, male counterpart of the High Priestess, introducer to dogma, orthodoxy.

Background—Just as nearly every society had a hierarchical ruler so did it have a head religious authority figure. He or she instructed the others in their mythology's initiation rites and mysteries. Of course this continues today and the Pope card's namesake still exists in the 21st century. Less formally, any figure who introduces a spiritual practice, body of knowledge, etc. plays this part in someone else's life.

Additional interpretation—The High Priest, and High Priestess, point us to something higher and greater than ourselves. In that way the Pope is somewhat a counterpart to the Emperor as his concern is the heavenly kingdom while the Emperor focuses on the temporal one. Back in 15th century Europe it was no surprise to see this figure outranking the Emperor.

Miscellaneous—Notice that the Empress and Emperor sit side by side in the major arcana but not the High Priestess and High Priest. This tetrarch forms a notable but overlooked block within the major arcana. It exists in the first 10 cards of the 22 which is mostly concerned with characters rather than phenomena. Additionally the first 5 (6 counting the Fool) were likely meant as a *ranks of man* section. This was a common artistic convention of the time where a cross section of humanity was portrayed in popular art, going from low ranking to high.[54] The first five numbered cards forming a special grouping was noted early on.

> "Of these the first five are called the Petits Atouts and the last five the Grands Atouts." *The Gentleman's Magazine Library* 1849[55]

Back to our pair of pairs in particular, they are 4 authority figures ordered in the following way . . . spiritual female, earthly female, earthly male, spiritual male. There is an interesting symmetry there. It results from the Emperor and Pope often being paired together in art of the time, representing the highest strata of society. The Empress being side by side with the Emperor makes perfect sense but not so with the Popess and her male equivalent, hence her placement as the first of the 4 card set.

The Lover or Lovers, VI

Fig 20

Consensus—A couple meets under the Sun and/or heavens. Common ascriptions include love, attraction, joy, choice, relationship issues including choosing between alternatives.

Background—Romeo and Juliet are just one pair out of an endless list of lovers from the popular consciousness. And how many celebrity or royal couples fascinate people today, and will in the future? This is a strong archetype including the trials and tribulations of relationships. Lancelot-Guinevere-Arthur is an archaic love triangle whose storytelling pattern still resonates today and we have 3 people, not just a happy 2, in the traditional depiction of this card.

Additional interpretation—The art of the early Lover(s) card is fairly ambiguous and can therefore be taken in different ways such as ... a lover making a choice between two potential mates, a marriage, an introduction of 2 future mates by a third party, a lovers' quarrel with a friend interceding, etc. However, the scene that perhaps deserves the top position as surface interpretation is the magic moment of first meeting a special someone. The cupid hovering overhead would seem most appropriate in that case. He is, by this interpretation, about to fire his arrow and strike the thereby newly smitten person in a folkloric convention that still exists today. If taken that way, then this card also speaks to clarification, finding the right path, person or purpose for yourself.

Love can be about more than feelings for another person and amorous or sexual attraction is not the only kind we experience. How often do we find ourselves saying we, "love" a book, movie, hobby or food? The search for or finding of joy in a broader sense may apply here as well.

Miscellaneous—A proposed inspiration for this card's visual is the Greek myth of Hercules once having to choose between 2 ladies, Vice and Virtue, at a crossroads.[56]

The Chariot, VII

Fig 21

Consensus—A resplendent charioteer stands in his vehicle. Common ascriptions include control, staying focused, victory and triumph, action in the world, movement towards a goal.

Background—The chariot was a divine symbol in many cultures. Symbolically it was the man made version of a pegasus, an earthly transport that transcends to the celestial. In many mythologies including Norse, the Sun is a golden chariot riding across the sky or it is being pulled by one. Helios from ancient Greek lore would be the best remembered example.

The earthly chariot was inextricably linked to glory with champion charioteers being superstars in Greece and Rome. Egyptian pharaohs were often portrayed riding one in dynastic art. Best remembered is the Roman triumph, the ritual wherein the leader who won a great military victory rode in splendor through the streets in a chariot, to the cheers and adulation of the people.

Additional interpretation—The Chariot must be taken in one of two major ways. He has accomplished his task or he is actively moving towards it. If he has accomplished it, the person seeking guidance may see this as a desired end state. Someone currently flush with accomplishments could see their present in the card. But there is always something higher to reach for, the chariot of the skies. And the skies are where spirits duel; there are spiritual as well as secular accomplishments.

Miscellaneous—A well-remembered tradition in those grand Roman triumphs involved the victor being constantly reminded that he was not a god with the mantra-like repetition of the phrase, "Remember, thou art mortal."[57] He would also then give sacrifices to Jupiter upon arriving at the Capitoline Hill. The higher the accomplishment, the more the need for humility.

Justice, VIII

Fig 22

Consensus—Lady Justice sits ready to weigh actions and make judgements. Common ascriptions include fairness, balance, judgment, cause and effect, truth, rules.

Background—Lady Justice, based on the Greek goddess Themis, has been a symbol for millennia and is still in use today from courtrooms to astrology (e.g. Libra's scales). The scales imply balancing so that the punishment is commensurate with the crime, a concept that goes back to earliest recorded history with the code of Hammurabi. The sword implies the punishment itself but as other authors have noted, in a Tarot context it is also the clear thinking that makes the judgment.

Additional interpretation—Our lady is far more immortal than mortal, unlike every card that came before her. In other words, there were real life fools, magicians, priests/priestesses (nuns), emperors/empresses but not female judges in European society at the time. That makes Justice's personification as a female notable despite the obvious classical Greek model. It also shows how the ranks of man section ended with the Pope, things then moving on with the clearly allegorical Lover(s) card. Compassion may have been an intimation of the female judge but her punishment was no less fearsome because of it. And judging comes at the end of a trial, literally and figuratively. Is there a trial of some kind that the pulling of this card relates to in a reading?

Miscellaneous—It is notable that the first completely mythic, central character in the sequence of 22 is a woman. Many have noted the preponderance of powerful, deific women in the major arcana. The artistic templates naturally used by a Renaissance artist make this far less surprising than many previous authors have stated but it is nonetheless noteworthy.

The Hermit, VIIII

Fig 23

Consensus—A wise, old man travels alone in search of something. Common ascriptions include inner contemplation, the search for knowledge and truth, isolation, asceticism.

Background—The Hermit would not have been a mysterious or unfamiliar character for the original viewers of the cards. He was often portrayed in various forms of popular art including in the *ranks of man* galleries discussed earlier. Those ranks in turn often appeared in *Dance of Death* works.

Fig 24 - One of countless versions of The Dance of Death.

This artistic tradition was possibly a very important influence on the Tarot as we'll see. In these works, Death invites all members of society to dance with him (e.g. die).[58] No one had the option to say no and the high level message was sometimes called the *Triumph of Death*. Those viewing these paintings or paper broadsides were thereby extolled to spend their time on Earth preparing properly for the afterlife. The Hermit was a typical person on Death's dance card. In one version, Death congratulates him for his readiness due to his spiritual focus during his time on Earth.

> "You may very well dance gladly, To you belongs the heavenly kingdom."[59]

The Hermit manages to touch on more than one recurring pattern in human thought. One is the wise old man, which is clearly a part of this card. Another is the hermit, hence his name, the person who removes themselves from society in order to attain enlightenment. Both are archetypes the world over. Sometimes the two aspects are present in one person and sometimes they are not. For instance, Japan's most legendary swordsman Miyamoto Musashi became a hermit late in life, retiring to a cave. But on the other hand the Buddha was not elderly when he did the same, separating himself from society to meditate in, coincidentally, a cave.

Part of this included the rejecting of comfort. The Hermit is an ascetic who believes the finer things in life keep us from advancing on our path to enlightenment. Even current popular entertainment highlights this archetype at times, martial arts movies being one example.

Lastly, the Greek philosopher Diogenes cannot go unmentioned as a possible historical precedent to the Tarot's wandering old man. Anyone from the Renaissance or beyond schooled in classical matters would have instantly made the association when viewing the card.

Additional interpretation—The Hermit's wise man aspect, shared by the Pope, makes him more Merlin than the Magician, whose more appropriate interpretation was already discussed. Incidentally, in Jung's formal archetypes the wise man and the magician are two separate entities.

As previous writers have noted, the passage of time was originally a well understood meaning of this card. He was early on depicted carrying an hourglass instead of a lantern, and was perhaps even an allusion to the god Cronus.[60] His passage of time implication is a useful facet of human life to add back into Tarot readings.

Miscellaneous—The aspect of the Hermit we may see less of in the future is the wise old man/person. Its unintended removal can already be seen in much current Tarot literature. The youth obsessed culture of today is little like bygone ones where age was venerated. In fact if you look at popular Tarot teachers online, the average age is sure to be much, much younger than the Hermit. And note the High Priestess was originally also depicted as well along in years. Both cards are important reminders that wisdom comes with time and many of our youthful opinions will be upended by the years.

That is not to say the young cannot impart wisdom or the old cannot be unwise. A bookend warning to the one about youthful overconfidence is age-based complacency. The Hermit is still searching with his lantern, still journeying with his staff despite his advanced years.

The Wheel of Fortune, X

Fig 25

Consensus—An allegorical spinning wheel represents the seeming unpredictability, from our perspective, of fate. Common ascriptions include fortune, fate, cyclical change, destiny, a turning point.

Background—A wheel naturally lends itself to interpretations of changing fortunes, cycles and unpredictable outcomes. Just think of many of today's casino games for an indication of that. It was a common symbol used in many medieval illustrations, these depictions clearly being precursors to the Tarot's version. While every entity on the wheel will fall and rise, a common lesson baked into these depictions was nevertheless that of fortunes falling. If you're up now, know that fate is likely to bring you low. This warning was a central classical ideal inherited by the later European society that birthed the Tarot. Many examples of the non-Tarot wheel of fate placed false or corrupt authority figures at the apex.

In those medieval images, a mythical lady was usually turning or holding the wheel. The concept of outcomes being determined by a female deity of sorts survived from the Roman goddess Fortuna into the same century as the casinos mentioned above. After all, it was Frank Sinatra who sang, "Luck be a lady tonight."

The wheel is also an important Buddhist symbol. *The Wheel of Life* represents spiritual change, transformation and rebirth. *Hecate's Wheel* is an ancient Greek symbol tied to its namesake Goddess and her triple aspect. And there are 3 creatures pictured on the Marseille depiction but one of the very earliest surviving decks, the famed Visconti, has 3 people on the Wheel. And the ancient cult of Orpheus, promulgated in ancient Greece by Pythogras no less, had a *Wheel of Rebirth*.

Additional interpretation—There is a lot of karmic warning in the Tarot. The Wheel bucks that trend as random chance is, possibly, hinted at regardless of it being fate's wheel. Even if someone or something mystical knows where the wheel will land for us, we don't. A lack of guarantee and a cautionary note about unpredictable results despite our best efforts could be read into it. The old bon mot that the only constant is change feels appropriate for this card. The Wheel is open to a wide number of interpretations, from a fated outcome that cannot be escaped to a random one, to one influenced by our actions. However, the concept of a low following a high was likely principally implied and worthy of renewed use today.

Miscellaneous—Despite the verbiage being a bit dense, an ancient story concerning a wheel of a different sort does a good job of encapsulating the complicated relationship of chance, karma and how we might influence the final result of even things that are fated.

"I went down to the potter's house, and, behold, he wrought a work on the wheels. And the vessel that he made of clay was marred . . . so he made it again another vessel, as seemed good to the potter to make it.

Then the word of the Jehovah came to me, saying. . . . O house of Israel, cannot I do with you as this potter? Sayeth Jehovah. Behold, as the clay in the potter's hand, so are ye in my hand, O house of Israel. At what instant I shall speak concerning a nation, and concerning a kingdom, to pluck up and to break down and to destroy it; if that nation, concerning which I have spoken, turn from their evil, I will repent of the evil that I thought to do unto them. And at what instant I shall speak concerning a nation, and concerning a kingdom, to build and to plant it; if they do that which is evil in my sight, that they obey not my voice, then I will repent of the good, wherewith I said I would benefit them"[61] Jeremiah 18

Force, XI

Fig 26

Consensus—A woman subdues a lion. Common ascriptions include courage, strength, sympathy, persuasion.

Background—Three of Christianity's 4 cardinal virtues are represented in the Tarot. And these 3 have been collectively called the moral virtues.[62] This card represents Fortitude which was its original name. The other two virtues are Temperance and Justice. In that context the card relates to perseverance in the face of trials and challenges, particularly moral ones.

This card is now interpreted as more related to strength and is usually called the Strength card. The force of will to stay on the right path despite hardships or temptation was portrayed as a woman controlling a lion which presumably represented untamed, animal instincts. The original inspiration for this visual was probably the mythical Amazon nymph and huntress Cyrene, who was seen by Apollo wrestling with and subduing a lion. One of the early versions of this card was by the way particularly superheroine in design, featuring a woman effortlessly breaking a stone pillar instead of controlling a lion.

Meanwhile strongmen, and gods, are common in world history. Hercules, Sampson, Melqart, Thor and Atlas are some examples. But it wasn't just men, even in the old patriarchal world as Cyrene and the Amazons indicate. Japanese mythology includes a woman with bone crushing power who effortlessly dragged a man off to her abode where she fed him rice with the consistency of stone, granting him great strength.

Additional interpretation—An early 20th century Catholic encyclopedia stated, "Hence fortitude, which implies a certain moral strength and courage, is the virtue by which one meets and sustains dangers and difficulties, even death itself."[63] As we'll see, the next 2 cards deal with death. Also, 5 of the next 6 can be thought of as dangers and difficulties, as can the previous card. This card's position in the major arcana sequence amidst or in preparation for cards that are thought by some to portray trials of various kinds therefore makes perfect sense.

Miscellaneous—A crucial component of this card is our animal nature. The original Christian view was that this needed to be subdued, period. A more evolved interpretation is that this card portrays a duality within each of us, both sides being necessary in a dynamic of give and take.

The Hanged Man, XII

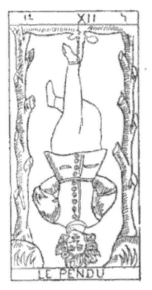

Fig 27

Consensus—A man hangs upside down, suspended from one foot. Common ascriptions include finding a new perspective, seclusion in order to gain insight, contemplation, pause, surrender, suspension of action, indecision.

Background—Today we read the title of this card in a genericized way. However, in antiquity the character on the card would not have been the Hanged Man but <u>the</u> Hanged Man. He is Judas, whose conspiring against Jesus was the quintessential act of betrayal in the European medieval and Renaissance mind. Early on the card was called, "Il Traditore" (The Traitor).[64]

Hanging via inverted suspension was a cruel technique and would result in a gruesome, prolonged death if the victim were left as is and not freed or dispatched in some quicker way.[65]

The depicted method of hanging references a humiliating form of punishment and/or execution associated with debtors and those seen as traitors.[66] The card's design is also a part of the *pittura infamante* (defaming portrait) artistic device which was used at the very nexus of time and place where the Tarot was created. You'll notice the lack of any of that in today's consensus interpretations of the card.

The contemplative qualities now ascribed to the Hanged Man should frankly belong to the Hermit instead. He is the one that consciously separates himself from the world in order to see things others do not and attain enlightenment. Some link this card to the Norse god Odin, who suspended himself from the world tree in order to gain insight. This is a misreading of the dynamic at play in this card in line with the consensus misreading that dominates Tarot literature. The Hanged Man is either executing himself (e.g. Judas hung himself) or being viciously punished. This is the only major arcana card that speaks to human treachery or betrayal and these are unfortunately common behaviors so it would be beneficial to reintroduce this aspect of the card to readings.

Additional interpretation—Judas hung himself because he finally realized the ultimate truth in a Christian context, that Jesus was God. So there is revelation, and divine revelation at that, in this card. This character did not suffer to then induce revelation (e.g. asceticism); he experienced a revelation and then suffered because of it. However, revelation is at least somewhat accounted for in common teachings. Along with betrayal though, the element of suffering is the obvious yet completely ignored aspect of this card. This was an absolute obsession for the religion and worldview that dominated European civilization when the cards were created. If the atouts can partially be understood as a map of life, then this is one of the stages of life along with the others seen in this part of that story. From a reading perspective this is not a pleasant but nevertheless valuable characteristic to add back into the panoply of prompts the Tarot provides.

Miscellaneous—Our character's facial expression is often used as evidence of his contemplative, peaceful nature. Actually this is more a function of art at the time. Contemporaneous illustrations often show people being tortured or devoured by beasts but with placid looks on their faces.[67] The noticeably odd position of the legs has elicited much commentary as well. Occultists have variously proposed that it is a symbol tied to alchemy, astrology, Buddhism and an Egyptian hieroglyph.

The Hanged Man does not look like someone who is hanging himself to death, does he? That's because the image, which has remained remarkably consistent, marries the 2 *different* descriptions of Judas' death from the New Testament.[68] It manages to do that while also emulating the cruel hanging method we discussed, which was also associated with use against a persecuted minority in Europe, the Jews.[69] That only reinforces the forgotten symbolism and its association with Judas in particular. This is all a far cry from the peaceful, self-improvement, meditating, yogi-like figure the Hanged Man is mistakenly described as today.

The Unnamed Arcana (Death), XIII

Fig 28

Consensus—An embodiment of death does his work with a scythe. Common ascriptions include end of a phase or cycle, transformation, transition, the end of something and the beginning of something else.

Background—

> "The preceding evidence shows that the effigy of Death is often regarded with fear and treated with marks of hatred and abhorrence." *The Golden Bough*[70]

The Grim Reaper has remarkable staying power in the popular imagination considering the agricultural metaphor he plays on is obsolete to most whereas it was a part of daily life centuries ago. Skeletons have also been their own notable character since time immemorial. Meanwhile scythes are a symbol of cutting down of course but also of reaping what you sowed, of realizing results. You only cut the crops down after the harvest has come in.

A personified version of death was an extremely common character and artistic convention. The artist who drew the first Death Tarot card could take inspiration from countless pre-existing models. And in those models he explicitly reminded people of everyone's eventual end, usually with a moral warning attached. This *memento mori* tradition is just one indication of how death was a prime fixation of art in Western society until very recently (relatively speaking). And this includes popular art meant for the common people.[71]

Additional interpretation—Most teachings go to pains to state that this card does not represent actual death. This is frankly ahistorical. It is inconceivable that people designing, making and viewing this card long ago did not think of real death when seeing it.

The Grim Reaper, by whatever name, is without question represented here and he is the ultimate personification of death in the Western world. Death was much more present in ancient times as well. Everybody in today's world will still obviously die but we are confronted with the loss of life much less frequently. A pandemic like the bubonic plague in today's world is practically unimaginable. The Center for Disease Control estimates up to 60% of Europe's population died during the plague.

Furthermore, today's society is rightly criticized for its inability to maturely cope with death compared to previous ones. And unlike today, those societies had important rituals and practices for actively remembering their dead. All of this produces the contemporary, comforting denial that the 13th card of the major arcana is not about the loss of life.

Death is as much a part of life as birth and this card reminds us of that.

What most of the present day lore correctly rails against regarding this card is the nonsense notion that pulling it means someone is going to die, die soon, etc. So how to rationalize (in the positive sense) it all? The consensus interpretations of the unnamed arcana are appropriate and philosophically valid. Death has been seen as a transition or gateway in countless religions after all. In that way another additional interpretation of this card is about mystery, going past a point of no return without knowing what is next. That can apply to our lives in many ways, death simply being the ultimate example.

Miscellaneous—Traditionally the Fool has a name and no number. This card has a number but no name. A common folkloric and religious belief is that there is great power in names and especially in invoking them (Yahweh, Rumpelstiltskin). The absent name could be interpreted as a sign of trepidation regarding the subject matter, reinforcing our interpretation of the card. Meanwhile the number could be as well. It is very unlikely this card was made the 13th by chance. The history of beliefs around that number is complicated. It was a very potent but not always negative number. However, it was thought of as representing evil as early as the days of the Zoroastrians.[72] Various reasons are proposed for why it eventually gained an unlucky connotation in superstitions. In short you could sum up our miscellaneous thoughts as . . . unlucky number-afraid to say its name.

Temperance, XIIII

Fig 29

Consensus—An angel pours liquid from one vessel to another. Common ascriptions include measure, blending, harmony, healing, even-tempered, balance, moderation, patience, purpose.

Background—Temperance is one of the 4 cardinal virtues in Christianity, 3 of which made it into the Tarot as previously noted. It is, "The moral virtue that moderates the attraction of pleasures and provides balance."[73] Temperance in general is about keeping things in balance and avoiding overindulgence. The pouring of liquid from one cup into the other is traditionally seen as the dilution of wine with water. The 20th century anti-alcohol Temperance movement even put statues of this angel's pre-Christian model, the cup-bearer goddess Hebe, in their *temperance fountains.*[74] Appropriate since the concept of temperance was inherited from classical Athens and important enough to Greek philosophy that Plato dedicates one of his dialogues to it.[75]

Additional interpretation—"The moral, I suppose, would be that the first requirements for a heroic career are the knightly virtues of loyalty, temperance, and courage."[76] So said Joseph Campbell in *The Power of Myth*. We may not associate temperance with heroism but we see in that quotation that it once was. Temperance is not only a matter of denying yourself something but of staying focused, in order that you may accomplish great things.

Someone doesn't have to be a Christian to take inspiration from the traditional image of the card which shows a divine force in the form of an angel at work. An extra additional meaning would then be to look for divine inspiration from whatever spiritual well a person draws from, to help keep balance. St. Ephren of Syria said, "Virtues are formed by prayer. Prayer preserves temperance . . . "[77] but that prayer or who it is directed to can take many forms.

Overall, the need for moderation may not be the most exciting reminder the Tarot provides but that does not make it any less important. In our current culture of indulgence it may even be more necessary than before.

Miscellaneous—Hebe was the cup-bearer to Zeus and the other gods on Olympus. As such there is the possibility of linking her or her Tarot visage to the Page of Cups should both cards come up in the same hand. By the same logic, any cup card in general may have a thematic link to this atout as well as the Star, which we'll get to later.

In the early evolution of the Tarot, the 3 virtue cards were moved around within the atouts more than any others, making strong interpretations regarding their place in the sequence challenging.

The Devil, XV

Fig 30

Consensus—The Devil stands or sits with two captives. Common ascriptions include addiction, materialism, empowerment, confidence, breaking taboos, primal desire, freedom from inhibitions, spiritual freedom, attachment, sexuality, darkness, temptation, passion, impulse, creativity.

Background—A medieval depiction of the Devil is portrayed on this card. Similar images from the time can easily be found outside of the Tarot, including carved into churches. Satan was the fallen angel who rebelled against God and then forever tempted humanity from the righteous path so they would miss out on heaven and instead be subjected to cruel torment in

Hell. This is of course Christianity's particularly drastic spin on a global pattern. Often there were separate but related gods of the upper and lower reaches (Zeus, Hades).

In the 19th and 20th centuries a veritable mountain of byzantine and contradictory occult theories were heaped onto this card. These usually involve interpretations that the figure is actually the theoretical deity Baphomet. This 'god' has left a very thin footprint in the history of mythology and religion at best however. The later, quintessential depiction of him/her as Baphomet by the hugely influential occultist Eliphas Levi has become the standard depiction and inspiration for the card. This significantly changes the symbol and symbolism. The image is much like the concept of Baphomet itself, a later fabrication that incorporates influences and elements as the creator saw fit.

Additional interpretations—This card may already have more widely disparate interpretations than any other because of the evolution discussed above. They run the gamut from being grounded to the original intent to being based on modern occult teachings which were in turn based on a syncretic blending of ancient beliefs.

That sentence actually applies to every card but it is starkly present here. Notice in our ascriptions the card is positive (empowerment, creativity, playfulness, freedom), negative (addiction, enslavement, materialism) and debatable (impulse, desire). The loosening of Christianity's dogmatic worldview is a part of this as passion, sexuality and other aspects were no longer seen as strictly dangers.

It's proper that the baseline meaning has remained intact . . . temptation or overindulgence leading to enslavement. That was Satan's work in the medieval mind but is no less relevant today. Drug addiction would be a classic example as the victim desires something to the point that it ends up controlling them, just as Satan controls the two people alongside him. Nowadays most have a more enlightened view about breaking taboos, challenging authority and accepting our animalistic side. Yet the path warned about originally is still valid. That is the inherent tension in the card which also makes it highly versatile.

Miscellaneous—In occultist teachings the Devil has been drastically changed, or rightly rehabilitated according to your point of view. In that sense it even becomes a question of whether or not this card represents the Devil. Some saw/see him as more of a Pan or Prometheus deity. Christianity's historical penchant for categorizing all competing gods as Satan or satanic has not helped in the slightest.

Regardless, the rebranding was done within these circles to the point where the goat headed (e.g. horny, sexual), devilish looking Baphomet even represents enlightenment and wisdom like a type of Western Buddha. That is neither good nor bad but did come much later and adds yet more complexity to the way the card is viewed.

The Tower, XVI

Fig 31

Consensus—A tower is struck by force from the heavens. Common ascriptions include disaster, upheaval, sudden change, chaos, revelation, discovery, transformation.

Background—Towers are mythically important structures as seen in fairy tales and elsewhere. They were a symbol of protection, allowing approaching dangers to be spotted and giving defenders a line of fire to strike at attackers scaling castle walls. Important prisoners and objects were put out of reach by being placed in them. They could also be seen as projections of seclusion, male power and the search for knowledge.

And yet there is ample agreement about this card's interpretation today. Upheaval or misfortune fits the image in both its (common) ancient and modern guises. It does however have a corresponding positive spin as seen in our ascriptions.

It should be noted that this card's visages and names changed more than most in antiquity including some showing a simple tower sans calamity.

This card taps into one of the most common myths, the natural disaster as wrath of the gods. The Old Testament of the Bible is brimming with them. The flood from Genesis was a reworking of an earlier eastern tale, tying it back to one of the earliest civilizations. Meanwhile Plato tells us that the gods destroyed Atlantis with, "one terrible night of fire and earthquakes" after, "the people had lost their way and turned to immoral pursuits."[78] Almost all societies in the ancient world interpreted drought, wildfire, earthquakes and floods as a divine punishment. Now however, to the exact background of this card's image.

> "Throughout history, when lightning did strike a church, many Christians believed that the lightning was evidence of divine wrath because of specific sins or heresies. Medieval and early modern Europeans routinely made this claim. Moreover, since the ringing of consecrated church bells was supposed to ward off thunderstorms and evil spirits, a strike was often regarded as particularly significant." The University of Chicago, Divinity School[79]

Lightning striking church towers was a fairly common phenomena in Europe because churches were usually the tallest building in the area and their towers, reaching toward heaven, were the tallest part of them. Also, the French name for this card translates as House of God. As if height wasn't enough of a problem, the towers almost always contained large metal bells that helped attract the lightning, referenced above. And we can get more specific still. The tower in our card is not part of a church. Was that just the original artist not having much room to work with? Emphasis added.

> "We recently took a look at a number of Churches with twisted spires. Rather more common are Churches with *detached bell towers*, though the architectural styles vary wildly. The most famous example is Italy's Torre di Pisa, more commonly known as the Leaning Tower of Pisa" Google Sightseeing[80]

Incidentally, construction on the (now) leaning tower of Pisa began in the 12th century so this type of construction was well known by the time of our cards.

The diary of a resident of Florence supports our hypothesis on the wrathful inspiration for this card even though the author describes strikes to cupolas instead of towers. Note that he was living in the country that invented the Tarot and at roughly the same time.

> "April 5, 1492: 11 pm . . . the . . . cupola of Santa Maria del Fiore was struck by a thunderbolt and it was split almost in half . . . November 4, 1511: And another struck the cupola of the Duomo, displacing about three niches, although they did not fall; and this meant some trouble for the Church . . . " *A Florentine Diary from 1450 to 1516* by Luca Landucci[81]

These strikes could cause minimal surface damage or total destruction via fire. This can still happen. A 200 year old church in Mississippi was completely destroyed this way in 2018. And what of the falling man/men in the original Tarot depiction? This could have been partly inspired by bell ringers. Remember that ringing church bells was believed to repel storms. This made bell ringer a dangerous job thanks to being tasked with manipulating the large, metallic objects at the exact wrong time.

Additional interpretation—The ambiguity about the card today is that the destruction from above can be seen as random or divine. In the former it is usually linked with the cards' purported ability to tell the future, which as a reminder I find entirely unconvincing. The reading of the card then becomes a warning that some sudden misfortune or change is on the way without cause. In the latter case, the karmic warning is clear and more profound. And this non-random interpretation is in line with the all but certain original meaning, a warning and/or punishment from God (the universe) about negative consequences coming as a result of negative actions. In this way the postulant is empowered to think of anti-productive behavior on their part that needs to change before consequences of it manifest.

Miscellaneous—Writers have tried to tie this tower to multiple historic or mythological ones. There is little doubt that many ancient users would have thought of the Bible's story of The Tower of Babel when pulling this card. Much like Atlantis, this structure was destroyed as a punishment for the people who built it. This nicely matches the overall mythic and specific historical influences outlined above.

Fig 32 - This 1547 CE depiction of the Tower of Babel's destruction quickly calls to mind the Rider-Waite-Smith version of the Tower card.

Another possible connection was first (I believe) noted by author Fred Gettings who stated a relief sculpture at the cathedral of Reims, France showed the Tower card scene.[82] The piece of art in question is actually in the Amiens cathedral and the image is part of a series there that seems to depict an alternate gospel legend where Jesus, Mary and Joseph arrive in Egypt and native idols fall from a temple there when they enter it.[83] This is a good microcosm of the difficulty in ascribing historic Tarot associations. There is a visual similarity between the Marseille Tower card and the piece in question but not so much with some of the earlier versions of the card. And even with the Marseille depiction, the similarities could be coincidence and that is not to say anything of the notable differences.

The Star, XVII

Fig 33

Consensus—A woman is channeling divine power or healing and sharing it down on Earth. Common ascriptions include divine inspiration, agent of the divine, spirituality, healing, sanctification, hope, purpose.

Background—This card is one of the more mysterious ones despite the conformity regarding interpretation. Renaissance art often featured a nude woman front and center as seen here. The Birth of Venus by Botticelli is a well-known masterpiece that comes to mind. It was created only decades after the Tarot's 15th century birth and in the same country.

Stars are divine. They were linked to the gods throughout history, even in the Christian era. A star led the wise men to the birth of Jesus. In *The Divine Comedy*, Dante states the celestial sphere where stars reside is 1 removed from the home of the angels and only 2 from God himself.[84]

The smaller set of stars in the image numbers 7 and various attributions have been proposed. Historically the most famous set of 7 stars in the sky is the Pleiades. In Greek myth these sisters were the daughters of Atlas who were transformed into the celestial bodies we see in the sky. Many cultures independently mythologized the Pleiades as females as well. The 8th star is larger than any of the 7 and could be Aldebaran, long part of the story of the celestial sisters in myth. If, and it is only an if, these are the 7 stars represented then we have a strong reinforcement of the female-deific allegory implied by the central figure. A small possibility along these lines is that the woman on the card relates to the story of a lost, 8th sister who did not ascend to the sky.

A better possibility is that she is an echo of one of the oldest of the gods, the Mesopotamian Ishtar-Inanna. Ishtar was associated with the planet Venus as her later Greek (Aphrodite) and Roman (Venus) counterparts would be, and her predominant symbol was a star. There are also various occurrences of the number 7 in regard to this star-goddess and her different cultural versions. Phoenicia's Astarte gave birth to 7 daughters and rode a chariot pulled by 7 lions. Egypt's Isis was guarded by 7 scorpion-like spirits. The 7 stars of the Pleiades were also the female hunting companions of yet another goddess, Artemis.

Additional interpretation—The enigmatic woman who takes center stage on this card relinquishes titular rights to the star. Should the star be our focus instead of she who usually dominates in card descriptions then? Or is she a personification of it on Earth?

In any event, the combination of water/liquid and starlight/fire here gives an elemental or maybe even alchemical aspect to the card. We presume the central character is acting down below on behalf of what is up above. The image calls to mind the Tibetan mandala once again as that object captures cosmic truth and is then shared with the world via water by being poured out into a river. A possible interpretation is therefore about taking something ethereal, making it tangible (e.g. real) and then sharing it.

Miscellaneous—There is more speculation and less certainty with this card's iconography than with most others. It has been linked to Sirius (Dog Star, the brightest in the sky), Venus and possibly more in addition to the musings above.

The similarity between Temperance and the Star is difficult to miss with the figures both using two liquid filled vessels, one in each hand. The balance Temperance promotes is mirrored by our star woman here despite the fact that she is pouring her libations out because she is doing so in equal measure. And that stays true even with the classic versions of this image where she is specifically pouring one liquid into water and the other onto land. Presumably this indicates earth and sea, in other words the entire world. Incidentally you'll notice that artistic convention elsewhere in the deck.

The Moon, XVIII

Fig 34

Consensus—The Moon shines above a placid scene of animals and architecture with either 2 dogs, 2 wolves or a dog and a wolf, each with a tower behind them. A body of water with a crayfish in it sits in the center. Common ascriptions include dreams, visions, receptivity, intuition, femininity, the unconscious mind, illusion, trepidation.

Background—This card is packed with as much symbolic imagery as any in the deck.

The Moon has been a source of fascination and myth in every culture throughout history. It was seen as a celestial body actively exerting influence down on Earth in a myriad of ways both physical and spiritual. It was also a deity, a place where souls go after death, the ruler of time (e.g. lunar calendar) and tides, influencer over human fertility and more.

Many including the Greeks, Romans, Mayans, Aztecs, Chinese and Mawu (in Africa) associated a goddess or female with the Moon. This card forms a pair with the masculine Sun, as the Empress does with the Emperor and the Popess with the Pope.

The Moon was linked to fear in some quarters, likely because it is associated with night and is progressively enveloped in darkness when waning. The darkness however hints at our unconsciousness or even the part of us Jung called *The Shadow*. Witchcraft was believed to be carried out at night under the auspices of the Moon. The eerie sound of wolves howling at night, or to the Moon, added to the air of unease that gradually overcame humanity's earlier, more holistic thoughts on it, at least in European culture.

Additional interpretation—The crustacean, either a crayfish or a lobster (they can be confused in ancient art) may be present due to natural behaviors that led to mythical associations, including in the zodiac.

> "Many species of invertebrates have behaviors that are timed based on the Moon's rhythms." *By the Light of the Moon: Invertebrate Lunar Calendars*[85]

Meanwhile, water appearing below the Moon is natural given its influence on the tides. A deep source of water is another symbol for the unconscious and the crustacean appears to be coming up from the depths to the surface.

There is a clear 3 part hierarchy at play in this card just as there is in the Tarot itself. It is no accident that Christians envisioned existence as 3 horizontal planes (Heaven, Earth, Hell). The Greeks (Olympus-sky, Earth, Hades) and countless others including secluded tribes did the same. Humans occupy the middle ground in these models (hence <u>Mid</u>gard). Appropriate then that only the middle card layer here contains evidence of humanity. This way of seeing the cross-section of all reality is embedded in the Moon card yet doubles as a mapping of a process of the soul, dreaming. The crustacean is not very relatable to us and its primordial design innately speaks of prehistory. It could then represent archaic patterns of the distant past buried within us as well as our own deepest thoughts. The much more relatable dogs (as I consider them) in the middle also look up. All eyes are directed towards the Moon. Speaking of dogs . . .

" . . . the dog has assumed a central place in countless mythologies as a guide between the worlds of life and death, known and unknown, human and animal, and symbolically between the conscious mind and the wilderness of the unconscious psyche and soul."[86] *The Book of Symbols*

The card is often linked to dreaming as mentioned and there is the obvious associative chain of Moon and night, night and sleep, sleep and dreams. It's also however because the card can be seen as a visual depiction of dreaming itself. Submerged thoughts rise up (lower layer) and are then displayed through visual metaphor (middle layer) to us during sleep. As far as the original Tarot is concerned, this is directed by a higher power (upper layer), the one that is pulling everything up. A final observation along those lines is that the droplets in this card are usually moving up towards the Moon while those in the next card are coming down from the Sun. Note- They are however both drawn the same way in the specific historic drawings reproduced here.

Miscellaneous—In the Marseille card, there is a Taoist, ying-yang theme to all 4 elements of the middle layer and their dueling similarities. Symbols from one side share visual motifs with symbols from the other in many older versions of this card. Sometimes the canine on the right for instance shares the color of the tower on the left and has one ear that is the color of the opposing canine, etc. A duality with the two elements at constant interplay is implied and this is not just a concept found in the Far East. It is present in many of the philosophies linked by some to the Tarot and this could be an indication of that. There is probably no way to definitively link the surreal imagery here to any one esoteric teaching but the goddess Hecate has been seen as alluded to in this card. Realistically, she is a goddess whose history and attributes have been so shifting and imprecise that it is a case of selective reasoning to make that association yet the speculation has merit. This triple faced deity is connected to the Moon, dogs, and dreaming after all.

"O Hecate, giver of light, send thy visions favorably!"
Helen by Euripedes[87]

The Sun, XVIIII

Fig 35

Consensus—The Sun blazes over two people, usually interpreted as children. Common ascriptions include masculinity, enjoyment, success, optimism, vitality, awareness, brilliance, rebirth.

Background—Like the Moon, the Sun has been a source of storytelling since the birth of language and thereby has innumerable mythical aspects. Principally it rules the skies as a male figure, thus kings and emperors long associated themselves with it. The Romans celebrated it as Sol Invictus, "The Unconquered Sun."[88] Sumerians pictured it as a man on a throne looking down, seeing all. In Egypt he (Ra) was the creator of life. He was the brother of the Moon goddess for the Muwa. The Celtic Sun god Belenus was also male, a shining conquering hero. The Sun wasn't just imposing though. It was also a source of comfort, banishing the dark of night, the cold of winter and making crops grow.

Today's very positive interpretations of the card are largely based on the Rider-Waite-Smith deck which radically reimagined it. Instead of an impassive faced Sun with two impassive looking people beneath, we get a natural (e.g. sans-clothes), smiling child riding a horse with arms thrust up in a celebratory pose, with sunflowers blooming in the background. Positive indeed.

Additional interpretation—It makes sense that the Sun card stands as the avatar of consciousness as the Moon does of unconsciousness even if that was not explicitly meant by the Tarot's creators. Things cannot hide in the glare of sunlight and the dawn reveals what was previously hidden. Also, the world at large wakes up with the Sun each day. That awakening can be likened to an intellectual one that comes from everything mentioned in this section, and that in turn fits with the overall process of reading the cards. It also fits in the pairing of this card with the previous one. The Moon card brought up what was buried. The Sun card can be the realization of what that was.

Miscellaneous—Unlike in the Moon card, the pair of beings here are not looking up but at each other. Their posture could be interpreted as one of assistance. They do not look as if they're enjoying a pleasant sunny day despite most associating them and the card with happiness. They may even be suffering from the heat, hence their sparse clothing. Then again the clothing could be indicative of their theorized young age. Seeing them as uncomfortable could also be a misunderstanding due to us looking at an archaic image as with the Hanged Man's facial expression.

Some say these two are happily dancing (in a garden, with all of the mythic tie-ins that entails). Others say they are the same pair from the Devil card, now freed or reborn. The Marseille pairs do look quite similar and one of the people in the Sun card seems to have a tail, like the corrupted people from the Devil card. Obviously there is ample room for disagreement about what is presented to the viewer, maybe more so than in most cards.

Judgement, XX

Fig 36

Consensus—As described in the Bible's Book of *Revelation*, an angel blows his trumpet and ushers in the end of the world, causing the dead to rise. Common ascriptions include reckoning, reunion, transcendence, rebirth, introspection, a calling from beyond.

Background—The Last Judgement is Christianity's apocalyptic myth. It is part of a larger and older tradition wherein the end of days or the current age is foretold within the context of a given belief system. Here, an angel announces the end as all manner of chaos breaks out on Earth. A third of the human race dies, a third of the land burns and a third of the waters are poisoned. Too many horrific miseries to name are visited upon the remaining population via the 4 horsemen of the apocalypse and many other agents.

The dead are raised from their graves as depicted, so they can be judged along with the living. This is much like other end of the world myths because it is the ushering in of a new epoch, "Then the One sitting on the throne spoke, 'Look, I am making the whole of creation new.'"[89]

Additional interpretation—The visuals in the card's original envisioning, even the earliest known, make clear that the emphasis is on resurrection and reunion, not death and destruction. The trumpet call therefore represents a proclamation that ushers in a momentous change. The sound of that horn/trumpet is an archetypal one if you will. Ram's horns and similar materials were used since prehistory for such purposes. They and their metal descendants could announce the start of battle or the arrival of a king. They called to the people and even to the gods in religious ceremonies. This card is partly about a call that must be heeded and after which nothing will be the same.

In *Revelation* the boundaries between the 3 layers of reality we spoke of earlier are breached. Just one example of that states, "And I saw an angel coming down out of heaven, having the key of the abyss and a great chain in his hand . . . "[90] Here you have a being from above coming down to the middle (where he captures *the* beast), with access to the realm below.

You could thereby layer in a meaning of shattered boundaries to this card.

Miscellaneous—The angel in our card is 1 of 7 who blow trumpets one at a time, usually ushering in a new wave of calamity, "And the first sounded, and there followed hail and fire, mingled with blood, and they were cast upon the earth . . . "[91]

Other commentators have noted the kinship this card has with Death as another end-beginning transition in the atout sequence. I'd call attention more specifically to the fact that if the unnamed arcana is in part a personal death, Judgement is the death of the world. This is partly what led me to describe the major arcana as a map of life, the world and the life of the world. The early cards can be seen as people and personal events (e.g. status, love, success, aging, changing fortunes, suffering). After Death the cards are *generally* more about the cosmos (e.g. world). The Devil is below in Hell, the Tower links to many myths of a large scale punishment on Earth; meanwhile the Star, Moon and Sun cards show the Earth and heavens. And then card XX ends the life of the cosmos just as Death ends an individual's. The wild cards here are the virtues and that is perhaps why they moved around in the sequence during the Tarot's development as mentioned previously. They are presumably included as qualities people should possess as they go through the stages of life. Exhibiting Justice-VIII prepares you for the judging that comes at the end of your life; this being hinted at by the old man/passage of time qualities of the Hermit-VIIII. Strength-XI (moral Fortitude) is needed to endure suffering, represented by the Hanged Man-XII. And Temperance-XIIII allows you to resist the temptation offered by the Devil-XV. We will wrestle more with the possible concept behind the trumps later. Just know that no hypothesis fits perfectly and there may be a good reason for that.

The World, XXI

Fig 37

Consensus—A woman stands framed in the center of the card while 4 creatures occupy the corners. Common ascriptions include completion, perfection, fulfillment, unity, journeying, exploration.

Background—The woman on this card reminds us strongly of the Venus-esque model we spoke of earlier with the Star. The card's arrangement is a *mandorla*, a central image in an almond shaped frame attended by 4 smaller images.

"The mandorla can be considered a Christian mandala because it is a sacred map of the world based on the essential representation of the earth, its sacred axis, which in this case is none other than Christ." *Metamorphosis: The Transfiguration in Byzantine Theology and Iconography*[92]

The mandorla framing device is a *vesica piscis*, a rich visual symbol itself born out of mathematics/geometry. It is created by two circles of the same size being partially merged so that a perfect almond-like shape results in the center where the two forms overlap. It was a feature of gothic architecture, a secret symbol for Christians during the 2nd century and much more.[93] Symbolically it could imply the melding of two opposing forces (e.g. the 2 circles joining). The pair could be male and female or divine and earthly among other scenarios, in any case making the vesica piscis a place of creation as something new forms in the center with attributes of both original forms.

The mandorla design is also cross-cultural as evinced by almost the exact same pattern being used in Buddhist art such as a 17th century depiction of the multi-limbed meditation deity Akshobhyavarja.[94] What is interesting about this card's mandorla is that it does not feature Jesus, etc. in the center as traditional Christian ones did. The figure at the sacred axis is instead our Renaissance nude, whose visual origins were taken from ancient Greece and Rome.

The Tarot's status as a game likely helped it avoid too much scrutiny and may be why a religious template contains a profane, by the Christian orthodox view, image in this card. Unsurprisingly, the Tarot did end up producing formal disapproval from the Church as its gallery of secular and pagan images combined with Christian ones offended religious authorities.[95] Playing cards in general were frowned upon by them because of their association with gambling as well. Tarot's use for divination greatly exacerbated the ill will as this was seen as heretical. As a side note it should be noted that the women in cards like the Star and World were modestly dressed in the earliest surviving Tarot representations.

Additional interpretations—The 4 corner creatures are subject to alchemical, astrological and other interpretations but their more probable origin casts the card in a different light. Historical antecedents notwithstanding, these entities are exactly what is described in the story of *Revelation* that we just covered with Judgement.

"The first living creature like a lion, the second living creature like an ox, the third living creature with the face of a man, and the fourth living creature like an eagle."[96]

The fact that this card comes immediately after Judgement puts this line of reasoning on firmer ground. The four creatures described above sit by God's throne and actually orchestrate the apocalypse. If the Revelation theme was intentionally continued from the last card, then the World represents the next world, the harmonious whole of creation made new after this one's destruction. The ability to create new life that women represent works well with this message as does the creative aspect of the *vesica piscis*. This Venus may be the new, unscarred creation that replaces the former, debased one. She is born naked, as everyone is, a symbol of birth but as a woman also of birthing. The life creation aspect may be indicated by the items traditionally shown in her hands. One is male (baton), the other female (container) and this fits precisely into the vesica piscis/mandorla device theme. Notice that this symbolism works even when she is not holding a container as in the specific historic version of the card reproduced here. That is because the woman herself is in that case the receptive female object and it is only the male principle that needs to be added. In either version, a thematic consistency involving male-female, creation of life, the vesica piscis and the previous card exists which is obscured in the popular Rider-Waite-Smith version of the card, where our nude is holding a baton in each hand.

Returning to our sacred axis woman, she might even be a creative mother-goddess or allusion to that general pattern, who in many pre-Christian systems was believed to have birthed the world. If so the card is a fascinating blend of pagan and Christian modalities the exact nature of which, like so much of the Tarot, can never be definitively proven.

None of this negates the common, modern-occult ascriptions above. But it brings the newness aspect to the fore and links this card strongly to the previous. It turns out that they form as much of a pair as the Empress-Emperor, High Priestess-High Priest or Moon-Sun. Together they also bolster the Tarot's cyclical theme where an end leads to a beginning.

Miscellaneous—The final card of the major arcana is a good chance to touch on how interrelated many of the cards are. This may or may not have been purposefully done with this card since it completes the set, at least in most decks (the Fool was sometimes 22).

- She, whoever she may be, reminds us of the naked woman in the Star.

- Her legs are crossed in the same manner as the Hanged Man's.

- The baton in this, the last numbered card of the atouts, looks very similar to that held by the first numbered card (the Magician).

- The angel on the card makes us think of Temperance and Judgement.

- There is a woman and a lion in this card as there is in Strength.

- The eagle on the card reminds us of the shields of both the Empress and Emperor.

CHAPTER 11

DO 22 STATUES TELL
1 STORY?

AT THE CLOSE of our last chapter we made it to the end of the trumps. Now let's briefly touch back on the start of the sequence as there is symmetry in returning to the first (Fool) after getting to the last (World), so we can consider the whole.

Today's understanding of the World card partly stems from viewing the major arcana not just as a purposeful, sequential story, but a particular one at that. This features the Fool as the protagonist of the tale. It is considered representative of every soul's journey from birth of consciousness to end of life and subsequent return to the universal. If the Magician is the start, the World must be the end of that <u>personal</u> journey. The *Fool's Allegorical Journey* is treated as canon today. And yet there is no historical evidence this was ever intended. To boot, none of the earliest surviving depictions of the Fool are even slightly flattering as previously noted. The homeless, deranged beggar/ entertainer who is harassed by dogs and children as he shuffles down the street would be an odd avatar for the everyman although flights of philosophical fancy can try to rationalize it.

As discussed in Chapter 10, he forms a pair with the Magician, another somewhat disreputable street entertainer. Side note- it is rarely if ever noted that the trump cards might all have been conceived of as a succession of pairs (see Appendix A). Anyway, the overlooked pairing of the Fool and Magician makes the Fool's supposed role as the special explorer who takes us through the rest of cards by experiencing them himself even less likely.

Fig 38 - *Facts and Speculations on the Origin and History of Playing Cards* (1848)

So there is no proof the Fool was meant to play the role Tarot orthodoxy places him in but then again there is equally no evidence that the major arcana or Tarot in toto was meant to be symbolically read or used, hence my phrase, *accidental oracle.*

Fig 39 – "Christ Descending into Hell" Jesus followed in the
footsteps of many predecessors by spending time plunging
into the underworld as part of his story.

And yet a link between the sequencing of these cards and
some deific galleries and initiation rites has been proposed.
Maybe these cards were created to emulate some specific version
of the overarching myth of the sacrificed and resurrected god
or hero (Jesus, Osiris, Orpheus, Persephone, Odysseus, etc.)
noted by Joseph Campbell and other scholars. Conversely
the similarities could be an unconscious manifestation of said
pattern in the psyche of the original designer(s). And then

again this or any other associations might simply be a product of the human penchant for striving to see patterns even in the pattern-less. In other words, it could just be a case of confirmation bias by later observers of the Tarot. Which if any of the possibilities spelled out in this paragraph is true? Short of a startling evidentiary find, we will never know.

This issue and the possibilities therein are a microcosm for all of the theorizing about the Tarot's purported hidden (occult) or overt (Christian) religious-mythological underpinnings. Some of the proposals are simply untrue but most are as intriguing as they are unsolvable. The Tarot is a relic found at a cultural crossroads and much of its faded ruins reflect that. The Renaissance was partly a time of new heretical ideas and images based on older, classical ones. Those in turn were highly influenced by various mythologies, foreign and domestic. And yet the Tarot was designed when conventional Christian thought and storytelling was still dominant, it also having links and precedents to many of the same older forerunners.

Is a nude woman in a mandorla a statement or an artistic choice devoid of message? We don't know but an uncomfortable likelihood is that the creation of the cards as a gaming instrument means the symbols and their sequencing were far more casual than assumed by generations of theorists and enthusiasts.

And still it is almost impossible to view the gallery and not see an allegory at play. Even some very dedicated students of the Tarot's history who reject any esoteric intention whatsoever see that. One line of reasoning from that quarter states that the major arcana was designed as an explicitly *exoteric* allegory, the type of which can be seen in much medieval and Renaissance art. This included the triumphal processions previously mentioned, at least of the religious or moral variety. The triumphal concept was a prevalent one and existed in many forms.

*   *   *

"But the Florentine Carnival surpassed the Roman in a certain class of processions . . . Among a crowd of masks on foot and on horseback appeared some huge, fantastic chariot, and upon it an allegorical figure . . . such as Jealousy with four spectacled faces on one head; the four temperaments with the planets belonging to them; the three Fates; Prudence enthroned above Hope and Fear, which lay bound before her; the four Elements, Ages, Winds, Seasons, and so on; as well as the famous chariot of Death with the coffins . . . Sometimes we meet with a splendid scene from classical mythology . . . Or else a chorus of figures forming some single class or category, as the beggars, the hunters and nymphs . . . the hermits, the astrologers, the vagabonds, the devils, the sellers of various kinds of wares . . . " *The Civilization of the Renaissance in Italy*[97]

On the one hand you have mortals, including from the lowest strata of society like beggars and vagabonds, which calls to mind the Fool and Magician. Notice that the hermit(s) is one of the noted character classes in the list as well. And yet the spectators also saw personified virtues (e.g. temperaments), death, inspirations from classical mythology, astronomical bodies and more. The similarities between that pageant and the atout tableau are obvious. Keep in mind the above is just 1 description of 1 location's particular processions.

You can also go from the big city to countryside villages and find much smaller European parades that tap into the same overarching processional form that may have exerted a large influence on the Tarot.

"When performed on Shrove Tuesday or Ash Wednesday, the ceremony of the expulsion of Death or Winter was pretty generally known as the Burial of the Carnival in Germany as well as in France, Spain and other countries of Europe."[98] *Journal of English and Germanic Philology*

This particular and widespread tradition, also called *burying the carnival*, varied from location to location. Notice how notable the following list of common elements from it throughout parts of Europe is in relation to the trumps . . . fools, priests, chariot, hanged man, death, resurrection.[99]

Aside from parades, contemporary artistic and literary traditions like the *Dance of Death* could also use the processional template. These could feature a similar mix of mortals the way the first 5, or 6, trumps do with the aforementioned *ranks of man*. As a reminder, many of these works featured the Emperor and Pope as the highest ranking pair, precisely as our cards do.

Many of these religious-folkloric celebrations and popular works of art focused on humanity, death and the triumphing over mortality and the Devil through Christian virtues, etc. Is that the exoteric story, the moral allegory that the 22 cards tell? A fair assessment must conclude this is a more likely possibility than their being a secretly encoded artifact meant to hide an arcane belief system in plain sight.

There are yet more candidates for the Tarot's still unknown ideological genesis playing off of this cultural motif. The most discussed literary source featured here is *Trionfi* by Petrarch (Francesco Petrarca, born 1304).[100]

Fig 40 - "Triumph of Love" and "Triumph of Death"
from the *Triumphs of Petrarch.*

If the designer of the atouts did play off of any of what was discussed in the last few paragraphs, the reason may have been fairly banal. The major arcana were originally unnumbered but knowing their order was crucial to gameplay as you had to know which ones outranked, or trumped, others. Using a culturally obvious sequencing of already well known visuals would be a great way to help players memorize the exact order of the cards. This book splits the baby as it were, recognizing a divinatory (but not fortune telling) validity in this relic while acknowledging the historically sound probability that it's design was pedestrian instead of esoteric. Non-esoteric does not mean the design lacks profundity any more than divination must equal reading the future. One definition of the word divination is, "unusual insight" and this tool produces that.

* * *

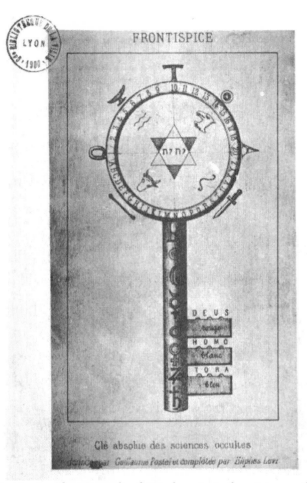

FRONTISPICE

Clé absolue des sciences occultes

Fig 41 - Another example of visual, esoteric theorizing on the
Tarot in the occultist tradition.

And on that note, none of the prognosticating about possible
original intent or inspiration changes how reading the cards
works, or the fact that reading them does work. The process of

using them in the eventual spiritual or psychological manner doesn't care whether the images started as a random collection of 15th century pop culture memes, a pagan pantheon, Christian allegory or something else entirely. So . . .

- Were the 22 cards designed to tell a purposeful story? Probably.

- If so, was the Fool meant to be the protagonist of that story? Almost certainly not.

- Did the major arcana inherit many conventions from popular, non-esoteric art and thought? Yes, in all likelihood the triumphal process/procession model in particular.

- Is it possible that alchemical, astrological or other concepts were consciously imbued into the design of the cards? Yes.

- Does any of this need to be correct for card reading to be an insightful experience? No.

Speaking of insight, I do believe there is a purposeful story or message laid out in the major arcana sequence. It is as obvious as it is overlooked and as overlooked as it is insightful.

Your life, like everyone's (ranks of man . . . Fool to Pope), will one day end (Death) after the ups and downs we all experience (Lovers-Chariot-Hermit-Wheel). Before that happens, you must choose (Pendu, Devil, virtues) how you will live out the temporary existence you have been granted in a world that is itself temporary (Judgement). Choose to live it in a way that is in harmony with the universe, its creator, its spirit (World).

That story may originally have been a simple mechanism casually employed. Employed that is to leverage the overarching biblical mythos of the day in order to make a game palatable to its intended audience. And yes, that itself may even have been a clever veneer of sorts for ideas outside of the mainstream. Regardless, the profundity of the greater message, unshackled from either an overt or underground belief system, remains intact . . . Will you use your time in a meaningful way or waste it? The Dance of Death reminds us that all who pass will do so with a sense of regret or fulfilment.

The major arcana is indeed a map of life, the world and the life of the world. The key is that the cosmic atlas presented to the viewers asks them to decide how their small journey over that vast landscape will proceed, and end. What story will it tell?

CHAPTER 12

MORE SACRED PLACES, MORE SACRED THINGS

W E TOOK A break from our overarching metaphor to tour the towering statues of the major arcana one by one and then consider the atouts en masse. And honestly those card by card considerations were partial views. An entire book could be written not just on those 22 cards but on any one of them. The many divergent views on possible inspirations and interpretations for them only prove how deep the well is that each of them taps into.

Now let's take a look at some other monuments and objects the Tarot shares properties with to better understand it as we close out our exploration.

We would be remiss if in that effort we did not mention China's classic fortune telling artifact, the *I Ching*. This *Book of Change* (or Changes) is the oldest of the Chinese literary classics. Its methods evolved into its current state about 2,000 years ago.

"This became the I Ching, the Book of Change, and its format has remained the same since: a named and numbered hexagram, an arcane "Judgment" for that hexagram, an often poetic interpretation of the image obtained by the combination of the two trigrams, and enigmatic statements on the meaning of each line of the hexagram."[101]

Users cast coins or sticks and then use the resulting numerical and geometric arrangements to determine which of the book's maxim's to consult. Consider the luck of the draw, combination of elements, visual prompts and inherited written interpretations. All of this reminds us of the Tarot. Also, the *I Ching* was progressively imbued with philosophical and religious ideas. In this case these were principally Confucianism, Taoism and Buddhism. That and the eventual use of the tool less for trying to literally tell the future and more for personal guidance also matches the Tarot's evolution.

Much closer to home so to speak, a sister tradition has been overlooked by most both in relation to the Tarot's origins and use. Catholic *holy cards* or *prayer cards* sprang up in or around the 15th century, like Tarot cards themselves. This is unsurprising as both grew out of the same European card making advent. It was natural enough for gaming and religious cards to be made simultaneously as there were separate markets for each. A 1430 reference exists where Antonio di Giovanni di ser Francesco mentions his woodblocks being sourced for the making of secular and sacred cards.[102]

Holy cards were pocket-sized devotional objects featuring religious art on one side and a prayer or biblical verse on the back. This tradition continues today and has fascinating similarities to the Tarot. These cards allowed what was previously unaffordable art to be possessed and carried by the average worshipper. By their nature these religious, visual, hand held objects focused on one thing at a time. These broadly boil down to Jesus, Mary, a biblical scene or saint. When featuring a person or deity as opposed to a scene, the prayer on the reverse was dedicated to that particular character. Each of those entities in turn had their own specialty for lack of a better word. One could ask for different things from different figures . . .

- Mercy from the Virgin Mary
- Strength from Saint Christopher
- Safety at sea (while fishing) from St. Peter

The list is almost endless. The similarity to our subject is clear but the exact nature of the connection will never be known. Did prayer cards influence the birth of the atouts, which then joined the four suits of playing cards to create the trionfi game? Conversely, did the major arcana sow the seeds for the creation of prayer cards; or neither? It seems probable that there was some type of cause and effect relationship here versus two completely independent but similar traditions springing up within the same general time and place. If nothing else, holy cards show yet another practice and sacred thing that the Tarot emulates. The difference is this is one may be a very close relation, either sibling, parent or child.

Religious cards were likely not invented by Roman Catholics. As Barbara Walker wrote in *The Secrets of the Tarot: Origins, History and Symbolism*, "Eastern peoples long used pasteboard picture-cards as unbound sacred books, to show the attributes of goddesses and gods, and to teach religious doctrines to children and other illiterates while they played games."[103] There is no prevailing theory that this produced the Christian version. The intimation by Walker and others is that they may have influenced the creation of the Tarot.

*   *   *

Capturing a two-dimensional archetypal image in a small format makes for easy carrying. The human need to visually express the ineffable however has no size limitations as some of the man-made sacred places covered earlier attest.

One version that we haven't covered strikes pretty close to home for the looming size we imagine our major arcana statues, windows or towers, sometimes having. The Buddha has been depicted in enormous statues in multiple countries. The Leshan Giant Buddha is considered the tallest ancient statue in the world. It was built around 800 CE out of a sandstone cliff face and is 71 meters tall.

On the other side of the Earth the Nazca people of present day Peru created geoglyphs so large they can only be appreciated from far above. These unique 2,000 year old monuments escape easy interpretation by researchers. The most well-known of the glyphs focus on single things like animals and plants. The largest of these measure an astonishing 370 meters in length. A 30 meter long mythical creature of some kind with many legs and an outthrust tongue also rests on the ground with more recognizable animals, all forever looking up. There are also many abstract geometric designs, something that was very present in the pre-modern Tarot deck minor pips but mostly absent today. Some of the straight lines running along the Peruvian plains are 48 kilometers long.

The Nazca lines are very old and their meanings lost because of that and the absence of written material left by their makers. We could say the same about the earliest existing sacred places of all. These are the Paleolithic cave paintings fortunately preserved due to their isolated locations. Some of the oldest known examples of these original cathedrals are 40,000 years old. The famous examples from Spain and France were a revelation for archeologists when first discovered.

They show that the need to explore and experience the great mysteries inside of an enclosed space has been with us since the start. Beliefs of many indigenous people make it a reasonable guess that caves have always held a mythic importance and not just because they were the earliest shelters. They were gateways to the spirit world and/or the land of the dead. This meaning survived into tales far later than Paleolithic man's day and can be seen throughout the world.

Many cave paintings are not found in easily accessible, surface level entrances just a few feet from the outside. The effort to create and worship deeper down with only the most primitive of lighting mechanisms speaks to the urge to worship in a cathedral before people could build one. The symbols found in the caves are the distant ancestors of every image found in a church, mosque or temple today. Speaking of examining ruins and making guesses in the dark, this is the height of it.

The visual discourse that happens with religious or archetypal images was of primal importance in the earliest of holy places due to the lack of any other form of communication. That kind of discourse still occurs with Tarot cards, objects that pull from the same fundamental forms as every authentic sacred place and object that came before them.

One epiphany related to the cave paintings came when the artificial light source archeologists were using in one of them ceased to function. Like the cavemen of old they had to use flame for illumination. When they did, they discovered that the symbols changed. Shadows covered some images while light fell on others. Two or more disparate images would be within the viewer's gaze and the mind would naturally form linkages. This could change with a flickering of flame or movement of the light source. A changing combination of mythic images in a sacred place; hopefully this sounds familiar by now.

We dealt with how the accidental oracle has a unique set of

features that tie back to the fundamental ways humans have created tangible objects to try and commune with the divine. It is not a stretch to say that we can add the original sacred space to the list and that it and Tarot cards share a mutability most others lack.

CONCLUSION

"I was in a house I did not know, which had two stories. It was "my house." I found myself in the upper story, where there was a kind of salon furnished with fine old pieces in Rococo style. On the walls hung a number of precious, old paintings. I wondered that this should be my house and thought, "Not bad." But then it occurred to me that I did not know what the lower floor looked like. Descending the stairs, I reached the ground floor. There everything was much older. I realized that this part of the house must date from about the fifteenth or sixteenth century. The furnishings were medieval, the floors were of red brick. Everywhere it was rather dark. I went from one room to another, thinking, "Now I really must explore the whole house." I came upon a heavy door and opened it. Beyond it, I discovered a stone stairway that led down into a cellar. Descending again, I found myself in a beautifully vaulted room which looked exceedingly ancient. Examining the walls, I discovered layers of brick among the ordinary stone blocks, and chips of brick in the mortar. As soon as I saw this, I knew that the walls dated from Roman times. My interest by now was intense. I looked more closely at the floor. It was of stone slabs and in one of these I discovered a ring. When I pulled it, the stone slab lifted and again I saw a stairway of narrow stone steps leading down to the depths. These, too, I descended and entered a low cave cut into rock. Thick dust lay on the floor and in the dust were scattered bones and broken pottery, like remains of a primitive culture. I discovered two human skulls, obviously very old, and half disintegrated. Then I awoke." Carl Jung, *Memories, Dreams, Reflections*[104]

Fig 42 - This was most certainly not the house Jung dreamt of; it is however a wonderful piece of imaginary architecture by visionary Jean-Jacques Lequeu (born 1757).

That was the dream or vision that led Jung to create his theory of the archetypes and collective unconscious. You can imagine how excited I was when I read that his dream's metaphor for the psyche was both architectural and archeological. Notice that the method of communication with it was entirely visual. No words were heard or read besides his own thoughts. His mind built a unique structure which presented symbols to him, which then led to a revelation. That building only existed in his mind and was destroyed that very night, never to be reconstructed again. How much of that can be applied to reading the cards?

Jung also had the means to later build an actual house that mirrored his thoughts, although not the one from that particular dream. It was a secluded chalet by a lake. He went there and, in the words of the BBC, ". . . withdrew into a place which was itself an expression of his own psyche in stone."[105]

It had an archaic design, no surprise there, looking more medieval than modern. He said of it and of building it, which he largely did with his own hands, "It gave me a feeling as if I was being reborn in stone."[106] He also said of it and of being there, "Here is space for the space-less kingdom . . . and the psyche's hinterland . . . Thoughts rise to the surface which reach back into the centuries"[107]

Over the doorway he had words from the Oracle at Delphi inscribed that read, "Whether called upon or not, God will be present."[108] Incidentally, he named this house the Tower.

Most of us won't be able to physically build a house that helps us get closer to God and/or our deeper selves. However unlikely it is, Tarot cards let us build one and an all but infinite number of them. The buildings aren't physical but we can imagine them as Jung did with the house from his dream. Explore deep enough and you can find revelations large and small. This book attempts to provide a new method for stimulating that exploration and in a manner that is consistent with the foundations and essence of the Tarot. As detailed, those foundations share traits with a myriad of practices and beliefs from around the world.

Let's conclude with one more of those. This is a spiritual exercise commonly called *deity yoga*, which was alluded to in our Introduction. This practice from Tantric Buddhism centers on the practitioner trying to identify with a specific deity. At a high level, the first stage of the process has the practitioner generate a complex visualization of the given deity's aspects and associations by envisioning its mandala. In the second stage this complicated visual construction is erased, just as real life mandalas often are. Scientific studies indicate that this exercise dramatically improves a person's *visuospatial processing*.

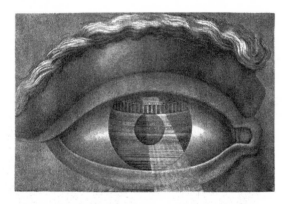

Fig 43 - *Eye Enclosing The Theatre At Besancon, France* by Claude Nicolas Ledoux (born 1736)

"Visuospatial processing is a fundamental aspect in human cognition, belonging to a complex and intricate network. It is, in other words, one of the building blocks of an individual's identity and behavior." *Visuospatial*

Processing: A Review from Basic to Current Concepts,
National Center for Biotechnology Information[109]

So it turns out this book's proposed way of understanding
and using the Tarot could add an unexpected benefit to those
who utilize it, one that goes to the core of our personalities.

Every coin has 2 sides and the benefits the cards provide
are counterbalanced by the danger they hold. They are not a
provider of easy answers. I spoke of confirmation bias when
discussing philosophical interpretations of the Tarot. Another
to beware of is postulants seeing the answer they hoped to see
in the cards or assuming whatever 'answer' they're given must
be correct. A tool of self-discovery can unfortunately become a
tool of self-delusion. And in the worst case scenario it is a tool
used for deluding others, done by those who peddle pretend
certainty in an uncertain world. The Tarot is fascinating on
a number of levels including artistic, folkloric, mythological,
religious, historical and psychological. It is also a very useful
and practical tool when properly understood.

There are epiphanies buried deep within us that may or may
not come from a higher power. Regardless, they are there and
the practice of the Tarot helps us excavate them. Hopefully this
book enriches that search.

"Man know thyself; then thou shalt know the universe
and God." Pythagoras[110]

APPENDIX A

A SUCCESSION OF SECTIONS

O UR CARDS HAVE been arranged in many novel ways by previous writers and users in an effort to better understand them. To be clear these are not spreads in the normal sense, not an arrangement meant for delivering a reading.

In one method for the major arcana, two rows are made out of cards 1 to 20. The top row contains cards I to X, the bottom XI-XX. The Fool and The World go on the ends of the resulting horizontal block, existing in neither row but in the middle ground.[111] The symmetrical shape thereby pairs up 20 of the 22 cards, one on top of the other. Interesting results include the top row being more people/character based versus the lower one being a collection of phenomena. You also get notable pairings like the Pope being over the Devil. Our 19th century image of a similar shape back in the main text showed the same application but in a different order.

A far more complicated arrangement is to create an infinity symbol with all 22 trumps so that cards XX (Wheel) and XI (World) meet at the intersection of the two circles. This *Wheels of Becoming* form as it is called produces many fascinating, potential connections.[112] Each card is paired with its opposite from the opposing circle, with their numbers always equaling 20.

Finally a full 78 card arrangement that is quite useful for taking it all in so to speak involves making a square out of the minor arcana which then contains a triangle made of the major arcana. This works out perfectly as the 4 sets of 14 of the minor arcana each make up one side of the square. Meanwhile cards 1 to 21 make the triangle on the inside, which contains the Fool who is the center point of the entire thing.[113]

But of the many ways to arrange the cards in order to explore them, the simplest may be the one that was actually used by the creator(s). Some pairs in the major arcana are obvious, Empress and Emperor, Moon and Sun, etc. However, it does seem like the entire sequence of atouts could be a collection of pairs. We know that the concept of trumping or triumphing is central to the Tarot's original design, with each major arcana card trumping the previous one. On that note it is interesting that you can, *conceivably*, see each pair we will deal with below as doing that to the previous pair as well. But let's focus on the actual pairings.

Fool – Magician: As mentioned, these are both street entertainers of a somewhat disreputable character. You could even say the first is taken advantage of by others whereas the second takes advantage of them. In other words, people arguably laughed at the Fool more than they laughed with him. Meanwhile the mountebank of a Magician conned those same people.

Popess – Empress: These are both female authorities, one spiritual, the other secular.

Emperor – Pope: This is a corresponding male pair to the previous female one, although in the secular, spiritual order. Interestingly, the Empress and Emperor also form a side by side pair while the Popess and Pope do not.

Lovers – Chariot: In the past, these cards have been linked as 2 success cards in 2 different areas, love and war. The military triumph the Chariot would have implied to many in the old world could be thought of as business today. Essentially the pair is about the personal and professional.

Justice – Hermit: These admittedly don't jump to mind as natural partners or differing sides of the same coin. Still, they are both seekers of knowledge, of truth. Justice is receptive, evidence and arguments are brought to her and she discerns the truth. The Hermit meanwhile goes out to find it.

Wheel – Force: These two form a surprisingly natural fit. The Wheel represents things dictated by a higher power(s). Force is the exact opposite with a person themselves exerting the control. There is a fate versus free will dynamic in the pair, or at least there could be.

Hanged Man – Death: Properly understood, the Hanged Man is dying so we have 2 mortality cards together. The difference is that in the first card, death is a choice made by man while Death itself is the one making the choice in the second.

Temperance – Devil: Living the virtue of Temperance through the exercise of moderation is the natural opposite of the overindulgence and surrendering to temptation that the Devil card can represent. A straightforward Christian theme and understanding is plain in this pair with the angel and the Devil offering opposite paths.

Tower – Star: Both of these cards are generally interpreted as showing actions of the cosmic divine manifested on Earth. The celestial plane brings down a calamity with the Tower, healing with the Star. Punishment versus forgiveness can be seen in this pair. Visually these cards may make a discordant couple but thematically they fit together nicely.

Moon – Sun: No explanation is really required here. It is most unlikely that these two cards are together in the major arcana sequence by accident.

Judgement – World: Once Judgement is properly understood, it's relation to the World card becomes obvious as detailed in our main text.

Luckily this prism for examining the cards is like all others in that it doesn't need to be true to be useful. However, if we want a pairing analysis that is 'true,' we have an option. That's because we know each card triumphs or trumps over the previous in the original design. For that reason you can walk through the sequence of atouts as a set of *rolling pairs*. In other words, consider them as . . .

Fool-Magician
Magician-Popess
Popess-Empress
Empress-Emperor
Emperor-Pope
Pope-Lovers

Lovers-Chariot
Chariot-Judgement
Judgement-Hermit
Hermit-Wheel
Wheel-Force
Force-Hanged Man
Hanged Man-Death
Death-Temperance
Temperance-Devil
Devil-Tower
Tower-Star
Star-Moon
Moon-Sun
Sun-Judgement
Judgement-World

Doing that gives you 21 pairs to consider, matching the total of numbered atouts. More to the point, thinking about how or why each card on the right can be seen as triumphing symbolically over its antecedent on the left gives us a new dimension to add to readings. This is of course just one more arrow in the quiver. Even if incorporated it doesn't have to dominate a reading of major arcana cards in a draw. But unlike template driven, positional interpretations and so many other standard practices today, this one is actually connected to the *known*, original conception of the cards.

APPENDIX B

QUOTATIONS

"In the 15th and 16th centuries, the exoteric symbolism of most of the Tarot trumps would have been apparent to all educated Italians . . . The presence of this exoteric symbolism in no way rules out that of a deeper level of esoteric symbolism needing specialized knowledge, not possessed by all educated people of the time, to discern . . . " *A Wicked Pack of Cards: The Origins of the Occult Tarot*[114]

"Let them construct a sanctuary for me, that I may dwell among them." *Book of Exodus*, 25:8[115]

"Destroy this temple, and in three days I will raise it up." Jesus Christ, *John* 2:19[116]

"In fact, the bad poet is usually unconscious where he ought to be conscious, and conscious where he ought to be unconscious." T.S. Elliot[117]

"The Tarot will lose all its vitality for one who allows himself to be side-tracked by its pedantry." Aleister Crowley[118]

"By the 1500's, the Italian aristocracy was enjoying a game known as "tarocchi appropriati," in which players were dealt random cards and used thematic associations with these cards to write poetic verses about one another."[119]

"The symbol is sacred because it is sacred. Meaning derives from that which happens to us when we see the symbol. Agency penetrates that symbol, there is something in it that is speaking to us."[120]

"Symbols emerge, grow and fade away in the course of history. No individual can make them, change them or destroy them according to a personal whim because it is a part of history."[121]

"That which is Below corresponds to that which is Above, and that which is Above corresponds to that which is Below, to accomplish the miracle of the One Thing." Hermes Trismegistus, purported father of Hermetic philosophy.[122]

"Yes, I know of the Tarot. It is, as far as I know, the pack of cards originally used by the Spanish gypsies . . . They are still used for divinatory purposes." Carl Jung[123]

"These cards are really the origin of our pack of cards, in which the red and the black symbolize the opposites, and the division of four . . . also belongs to the individuation symbolism. They are psychological images, symbols with which one plays, as the unconscious seems to play with its contents. They combine in certain ways, and the different combinations correspond to the playful development of events in the history of mankind . . . besides, there are twenty-one cards upon which are symbols, or pictures of symbolical situations. For example, the symbol of the Sun, or the symbol of the man hung up by the feet, or the tower struck by lightning, or the wheel of fortune, and so on. Those are sort of archetypal ideas, of a differentiated nature, which mingle with the ordinary constituents of the flow of the unconscious, and therefore it is applicable for an intuitive method that has the purpose of understanding the flow of life, possibly even predicting future events, at all events lending itself to the reading of the conditions of the present moment. It is in that way analogous to the I Ching, the Chinese divination method that allows at least a reading of the present condition. You see, man always felt the need of finding an access through the unconscious to the meaning of an actual condition." Carl Jung, 1933[124]

"(Freud) knew the unconscious is far greater and older than the conscious, it thinks in mythical, magical and religious ways . . . it's the persistence in us of the archaic religious mind."[125]

"Archaic Heritage: phylogenetic remnants of the species' mental functioning such as inherited dispositions, ideational contents, and memory traces from former generations."[126]

"Freud was also an avid collector of antiquities. "The psychoanalyst," he said to an early patient famously dubbed the Wolf Man, "like the archaeologist in his excavations, must uncover layer after layer of the patient's psyche, before coming to the deepest, most valuable treasures." . . . by the time of his death . . . he had also managed to amass over 2,000 physical treasures from ancient kingdoms in Egypt, Greece, Rome, India, China, and Etruria." *How Sigmund Freud's Art Collection Influenced His Theories* - Artsy[127]

"Myths are clues to the spiritual potentialities of the human life." Joseph Campbell[128]

"Read myths. They teach you that you can turn inward, and you begin to get the message of the symbols." Joseph Campbell[129]

"Tarot is a card-game that you don`t play to win or lose. If there is a winner, it's the player who discovers the value of play itself." Philippe St Genoux[130]

"The true Tarot is symbolism; it speaks no other language and offers no other signs." A.E. Waite[131]

"Sublimity and tranquility are not thought of as natural companions, until that is you walk into a cathedral. Notre Dame is in a way the cathedral of cathedrals." Stephen Metcalf[132]

". . . as my eyes grew accustomed to the light, details of the room within emerged slowly from the mist, strange animals, statues, and gold - everywhere the glint of gold. For the moment - an eternity it must have seemed to the others standing by - I was struck dumb with amazement, and when Lord Carnarvon, unable to stand the suspense any longer, inquired anxiously, 'Can you see anything?' it was all I could do to get out the words, 'Yes, wonderful things."

Howard Carter, *The Path to Tutankhamen*[133]

APPENDIX C

THE ALMOST
INFINITE SPREAD

IN CHAPTER 6 we identified that a 39 card draw gives us the largest possible number of unique combinations (as opposed to permutations) and how the prospect of creating one beckoned. I am unaware of anyone previously creating such a spread, much less for this specific reason. Well why not? There are so many ways to approach this but here is mine; create a mandorla. That pattern after all ends the major arcana itself.

In my opinion constructing a Tarot spread should not feel like assembling a large piece of furniture with constant referencing back and forth to a complicated instruction manual. Therefore the process below is as straightforward as possible. That being said there is a slight bit of intricacy involved but only what is necessary.

Creation:

1. Place a card in the center of your space.

2. Create the vesica piscis around it with 30 cards, 15 on each side.

3.   Draw 4 cards and place them at the 4 corners outside of the almond frame.

4.   Draw 4 more cards and place them at the North, South, East and West positions. These represent the boundaries of a physical card itself. In other words they draw the edges of our space that normally the sides of the card do. For that reason the *inner* edge of each of them should be on the same imaginary line as the *outer* edge of the corresponding corner cards. They actually sit outside of the mandorla if you will.

Possible Interpretation:

The center card is the central figure of the arrangement, the sacred axis around which everything else exists. This represents the querent.

Remember that the vesica piscis represents two different forces coming together and creating something, in this case the querent themselves. The reader and querent can assign values to each of the two sides as suits the particular reading (mother-father, physical-spiritual, conscious-unconscious, passion-obligation, etc.). The point is that the two sides represent a duality that got them to where they now are as a person.

The 4 corner creatures can be thought of as active agents, which matches the historical basis of the original images as previously discussed. These are 4 things that can assist the querent in getting to where they need to be. The other 4 are constraining forces. They are the things, people or circumstances that inhibit the growth or rebirth that the overall spread represents.

And there you have it. 39 cards but really only 5 elements

1. querent
2. creative force 1
3. creative force 2
4. assisting forces
5. constraining forces

Variations:

Well everything above is merely a suggestion. However I do find it to be a method that is challenging yet fairly simple and intuitive, at least for a spread that large. Speaking of intuition there is ample room for it while still giving the positions of the cards some specificity.

Now if this is found to be a useful layout and approach, here are some ways to change it up while keeping to the overall plan.

- Use major arcana cards only for the central card.
- Use major arcana cards only for the central and 4 corner cards.
- Use major arcana cards only for the central, 4 corner and 4 boundary cards.
- Use only pip cards for the vesica piscis.
- Use only court cards for the 4 boundaries.

It is easy enough to incorporate any of the above variations without having to separate the deck into constituent parts. Just draw from the shuffled deck until you find the right number of desired card types and then continue with the process. Then again, 2 (major arcana and minor) or 3 (major arcana, court, pip) shuffled mini decks would work as well.

Use any of the above variations in any combination desired and/or invent your own. It should be noted that all of those, or any you think up yourself, change the ... purity ... of the probabilities that gave birth this idea in the first place. It's true that drawing straight from the deck with no limits as to what kind of card can sit where is the way to truly tap into the largest number of combinations possible. It is also the most challenging way to do a reading with this spread.

APPENDIX D

AN EXAMPLE IN CONCRETE

It's difficult to describe the experience of successfully creating and entering an imagined building based on a pull of the cards. This is especially true for a complex spread where the difficulty is greater but so consequently is the reward. I pulled a remarkable set of cards during the writing of this book and the resulting ethereal edifice is my favorite to date.

Luckily I was reading for myself at the time or it might not feel right to consider this one my favorite. I had pulled 12 cards in a semi-circle pattern, what Jodorowsky calls the *reduced spread*. In it there are no positional assignments, you just read the cards from left to right and each card adds meaning to the one that follows. By keeping the parabola symmetrical you get the center two cards (6 and 7) at top-center and the overall shape moving up and then down from the apex. Basically it is an arch or a dome and that fits our purposes just fine. Here are the cards that came out in a humble approximation of the shape . . .

Sun, 2 of Swords

Emperor   6 of Cups

Ace of Coins   Ace of Batons

King of Swords   Chariot

King of Cups   5 of Cups

Ace of Cups   Ace of Swords

Visualizing the spread as proposed in this book made the symmetry and symbolism of the cohesive whole stand out much more than had I not thought of it all spatially. All 4 aces are present but on top of that they are in matching positions, being the 1st, last, 4th and 4th to last cards in the spread as seen above. Understanding the odds of getting the cards that presented themselves added to the appreciation of how, well, special this arrangement was. The odds of getting the 12 given cards are 1 in 43 trillion. I do not know how to begin calculating the odds of getting all 4 aces in a pull of 12, out of a set of 78, much less getting them in matching positions. I can say they're truly astronomical. It is all but certain that this will never happen again. I might be the only person in history to ever get this exact hand.

Understanding that makes building it much more compelling but was that effort necessary? After all it was an entirely separate task to add to the already daunting one of finding meaning and a story in that long sequence of cards. And it certainly is easy to appreciate the art and beauty of a Tarot spread as is. So no, it's not necessary. I didn't need it but I can also say there is no comparing the actual visual of the cards on the table (I still have a picture of it) to the imagined building that ended up using them as a blueprint.

We won't be taking off on a linguistic flight of fancy in describing my translation of these cards into stone. To me this really is all about a practical mental exercise. But a simple tour is in order.

I ended up imagining a long white, great hall of a building made up of 11 sections, 5 on each side of a large, central swelling. White was the baseline color as it is the predominant background color in Marseille cards. The particular deck I used was fairly new so the white was bright and clear. If they were old and faded then maybe the walls would have been as well. Very tall walls ultimately come together in a sharp arch. Vertical, slit-like windows run along the sides and each terminate in a point, mimicking the overall cross-section of the building. The two sections on the ends were the Ace of Cups and Ace of Swords. The order of what you encounter from each end as you work your way inward is of course set by the cards. Each of the 10 outer cards was a three-dimensional representation of its subject.

The prominent center section is round and capped by a massive dome with a round portal at the center-top. The Sun shines directly over that and its light consequently falls straight down upon a garden tableau of sorts where the vegetation is entwining itself along two crossed swords. And obviously that is the union of the 2 central cards of the spread, the fulcrum.

The Ace of Cups is one of my favorite cards and I'm a big fan of the traditional Marseille representation that looks almost like a castle, a church and a mosque combined and then rendered into an ornate fountain standing in a vast body of water. So that fountain was there much as a holy water fountain is first encountered upon entering a Christian church. The water that flows out of that cup pools on the ground as in the card but also ends up dripping from above into the 2 different sets of cups found on the opposite side of the building (6 and 5 of Cups). And yet it's the same water that resides in the vessel held by the King of Cups.

The water acting in that magical-realist fashion was one way to associate different cards that have something in common. That's the kind of imaginative challenge that results from working through this as opposed to just knowing the 4 cup cards in the spread are of the same suit. I'll spare further details but linkages of other motifs can be seen elsewhere, colors, thrones and crowns in part but especially the flower/vine flourishes that appear on many of the cards and are prominent in the Ace of Swords.

Back to the 4 aces, they are large monuments that divide the overall longitudinal building into larger sections. That made sense because to me the whole spread is based on their presence and even distribution, which is what caught my attention in the first place.

Well, hopefully you can see how the exercise can just keep going if someone wants it to once they get started. You add an air of 3 dimensional exploration and imaginative creation to reading a spread that just does not exist otherwise.

Lastly, I've stressed repeatedly the danger of taking Tarot rules too strictly or seriously. The same applies to my method. There is no end to how someone might choose to visualize based on the cards, using the logic but not particulars of my approach. I do it myself. I drew a simple 3 card draw that encapsulated the last few years of my life. . . . Death, Magician, World. This was with a modern deck using the Marseille template but with more whimsical visuals. Death did his work on a hill, under a starry sky. I imagined an old graveyard on a hilltop at night (Death). On top was a small circus tent the likes of which would have been used by a travelling performer in centuries past (Magician). Inside, a spotlight illuminated our mysterious World woman. So I did stick to a physical structure but intuited far out of bounds of my usual choices.

ILLUSTRATIONS AND PHOTOS

32 *Fall of the Tower of Babel* by Cornelis Anthonisz (1547)

33-37 Cards XX-XXI, mostly from Le Tarot Des Bohemiens (1900)

38 *Facts and Speculations on the Origin and History of Playing Cards* (1848)

39 "Christ Descending into Hell," *A Loan Exhibition of Early Italian Engravings (intaglio): Fogg Art Museum* (1915)

40 Composite image made by author - "Triumph of Love, Triumph of Death from Triumphs of Petrarch," *A Loan Exhibition of Early Italian Engravings (intaglio): Fogg Art Museum* (1915)

41 Le Tarot Des Bohemiens (1889)

42 Illustration by Jean-Jacques Lequeu (born 1757)

43 Illustration by Claude Nicolas Ledoux (born 1736)

CITATIONS

Note- As much information as possible was provided about sources. Page number and other details are not always available due to source format (e.g. online scans, etc.).

1. "The Poetry of Light: 10 Quotes on Minimalism," architizer.com, https://architizer.com/blog/inspiration/industry/10-quotes-on-minimalism-by-tadao-ando/.

2. Andrew Hallahan, "Acting On the Path to Awakening: A Cognitive Exploration of Identity Transformation and Performance in Vajrayana Deity-Yoga" (Colorado College, 2015), https://digitalccbeta.coloradocollege.edu/pid/coccc:11176/datastream/OBJ.

3. M. Papus, *The Tarot of the Bohemians* as quoted in *Ars Quatuor Coronatorum* (Freemasons Lodge No. 2076, London), 189.

4. "The Tarot and other Early Cards," Andy's Playing Cards.com, http://l-pollett.tripod.com/cards64.htm.

5. Catherine Perry Hargrave, *A History of Playing Cards and a Bibliography of Cards and Gaming* (Dover: Dover Publications, 2012), 6.

6. May King, Mrs. J. K. Van Rensselaer Van Rensselaer, *The Devil's Picture-books. A History of Playing Cards* (New York: Dodd, Mead and Company, 1893).

7. Hunter Oatman-Stanford, "Tarot Mythology: The Surprising Origins of the World's Most Misunderstood Cards," collectorsweekly.com, https://www.collectors weekly.com/articles/the-surprising-origins-of-tarot-most-misunderstood-cards/.

8. "Origins of Cartomancy (Playing Card Divination)," Mary K. Greer's Tarot Blog, https://www.google.com/amp/s/marykgreer.com/2008/04/01/origins-of-divination-with-playing-cards/amp/.

9. Ronald Decker, Thierry Depaulis & Michael Dummett, *A Wicked Pack of Cards: The Origins of the Occult Tarot* (New York: St. Martin's Press, 1996).

10. *Journal of the Society of the Arts*, 1889.

11. Helen Farley, *Cultural History of Tarot: From Entertainment to Esotericism* (London: Tauris, 2009), 13.

12. May K. Greer, *Tarot for Your Self: A Workbook for Personal Transformation* (Franklin Lakes: New Page Books, 2002), 274.

13. Victor Hugo, *The Hunchback of Notre Dame* (1831), 75.

14. Peter Green, *The Greco-Persian Wars* (Berkeley: University of California Press, 1996), 95.

15. Alejandro Jodorowsky and Marianne Costa, *The Way of Tarot: The Spiritual Teacher in the Cards* (Rochester: Destiny Books 2009).

16. Rachael Nuwer, "This Japanese Shrine Has Been Torn Down And Rebuilt Every 20 Years for the Past Millennium," Smithsonian.com, https://www.smithsonianmag.com/smart-news/this-japanese-shrine-has-been-torn-down-and-rebuilt-every-20-years-for-the-past-millennium-575558/.

17. Hila Ratzabi, "What was the Tabernacle (Mishkan)?," myjewishlearning.com, https://www.myjewishlearning. com/article/the-tabernacle/.

18. David Macintosh, "Philosophy Now: A Magazine of Ideas Plato: A Theory of Forms," philosophynow.org, https:// philosophynow.org/issues/90/Plato_A_Theory_of_ Forms.

19. Par M. Court De Gebelin, *Monde Primitif* (Paris: De Diverses Academies Censur Royale, 1781).

20. Ibid.

21. *Carl Jung, The Archetypes and the Collective Unconscious Volume 9 Part I*, ed. Michael Fordham, M.D., M.R.C.P., and Gerhard Adler, Ph.D. Routledge London 1968.

22. Allan Silverman, "Stanford Encyclopedia of Philosphy Plato's Middle Period Metaphysics and Epistemology," https://plato.stanford.edu/entries/plato-metaphysics/.

23. Josh Jones, "Carl Jung: Tarot Cards Provide Doorways to the Unconscious, and Maybe a Way to Predict the Future," openculture.com, http://www.openculture. com/2017/08/carl-jung-tarot-cards-provide-doorways- to-the-unconscious-and-even-a-way-to-predict-the- future.html.

24. Jungianthology podcast, "Facing the Gods: Archetypal Patterns of Existence," John Van Eenwyk, Ph.D. in religion and psychology.

25. Michael Fordham, M.D., M.R.C.P., and Gerhard Adler, Ph.D., eds. *Carl Jung, The Archetypes and the Collective Unconscious Volume 9 Part I* (London: Routledge, 1968), 5.

26. William Blake, *The Marriage of Heaven and Hell* (1793).

27. Immanuel Kant, *Prolegomena* (1783).

28. Will Durant, *The Story of Philosophy* (New York: Simon and Schuster, 1961), 98.

29. Iamblichus of Chalcis, *Life of Pythagoras* (c. 300), as translated by Thomas Taylor (1818), wikiquote https://en.wikiquote.org/wiki/Pythagoras.

30. "Pythagoras and the Pythagoreans," Texas A&M University, https://www.math.tamu.edu/~don.allen/history/pythag/pythag.html.

31. Alejandro Jodorowsky, *L'Art Du Tarot* (Marseille, France). A longstanding Tarot tradition is the inclusion of an instructional booklet in the box that carries a set of cards. *L'Art Du Tarot* comes with Mr. Jodorowsky and Philip Caimon's version of the Marseille deck.

32. The Bible, Revelation 11:1.

33. "About How Many Stars are in Space?," UC Santa Barbara Science Line, https://scienceline.ucsb.edu/getkey.php?key=3775.

34. "Churchill and the Commons Chamber," parliament.uk, https://www.parliament.uk/about/living-heritage/building/palace/architecture/palacestructure/churchill/www.parliament.uk.

35. "Heraclitus Stanford Encyclopedia of Philosophy," Stanford.edu, https://plato.stanford.edu/entries/heraclitus/.

36. David Warburton *Architecture, Power, and Religion: Hatshepsut, Amun & Karnak in Context*, (LIT Verlag, 2012).

37. Ibid.

38. Elif Batuman, "The Myth of the Megalith," *The New Yorker* Dec 18, 2014.

39. Henry Matthews, *Being the Journal of a Tour in Pursuit of Health in Portugal, Italy, Switzerland, and France in the Years 1817, 1818, and 1819*, (London: W. Galignani and Co., 1836), 74.

40. Charlotte Anne Eaton, *Rome In the Nineteenth Century, Vol 1* (London: George Bell & Sons, 1817).

41. Sir James Frazer Wordsworth, *The Golden Bough* (Hertfordshire: Reference, 1993), 593-594.

42. Jill Badonsky, *The Muse Is In: An Owner's Manual to Your Creativity* (Philadelphia: Running Press, 2013).

43. Jungianthology podcast, "Facing the Gods: Archetypal Patterns of Existence," John Van Eenwyk, Ph.D. in religion and psychology.

44. "ineffable," oxford dictionaries, https://en.oxford dictionaries.com/definition/ineffable.

45. Philebus, *Tarocchi: Introducing the Card Games for Tarot* (CreateSpace Independent Publishing Platform, 2009), 17.

46. Robert M. Place, *The Tarot: History, Symbolism, and Divination* (New York: Penguin, 2005).

47. "IL MATTO - THE FOOL," tarotwheel.net, http://tarot wheel.net/history/the%20individual%20trump%20cards/ il%20matto%20-%20the%20fool.html.

48. Cynthia Giles, *The Tarot: History, Mystery and Lore* (New York: Simon and Schuster, 1992), 16.

49. "Franco Pratesi: Playing Card Researches 2011/12, mainly in Florence," trionfi.com, http://trionfi.com/franco-pratesi.

50. George Hart Routledge, *The Routledge Dictionary of Egyptian Gods and Goddesses* (London: Routledge, 2005).

51. Michael J. Hurst, "Popess: The Exemplary Mode," pre-Gebelin tarot history.com,_http://pre-gebelin.blogspot. com/2012/08/popess-exemplary-mode.html.

52. Cynthia Giles, *The Tarot: History, Mystery and Lore* (New York: Simon and Schuster, 1992), 16.

53. "Empress," Cambridge.com, https://dictionary.cambridge. org/us/dictionary/english/empress.

54. Michael J. Hurst, "Gallery: Ranks of Mankind," pre-Gebelin tarot history.com,_http://pre-gebelin.blogspot. com/2013/02/gallery-ranks-of-mankind.html.

55. George Gomme, ed. *The Gentleman's Magazine Library: A Classified Collection of the Chief Contents of The Gentleman's Magazine from 1731-1868* (London: Elliot Stock, 1889), 174.

56. Arthur Asa Berger, *Media, Myth, and Society* (New York: Palgrave McMillan, 2013).

57. Valerie A. Maxfield, *The Military Decorations of the Roman Army* (Berkeley: University of California Press, 1981), 102.

58. "Dance of Death," dodedans.com, http://www.dodedans. com/Eindex.htm.

59. "Lubeck's Dance of Death," dodedans.com, http://www. dodedans.com/Etext8.htm.

60. "Hermit with Hourglass," tarotforum.net-Aeclectic Tarot forum, http://www.tarotforum.net/showthread. php?p=1347652.

61. The Bible, Jeremiah 18.

62. Michael J. Hurst, "The Three Moral Virtues,"pre-Gebelin tarot history.com http://pre-gebelin.blogspot. com/2008/04/moral-virtues.html.

63. "Virtue," newadvent.org, http://www.newadvent.org/cathen/15472a.htm.

64. Robert Place, *The Fool's Journey: The History, Art, and Symbolism of the Tarot* (Saugerties: Talarius Publications, 2010), 81.

65. Michael J. Hurst, "A Modern Catholic Looks at Tarot," pre-Gebelin tarot history.com,_http://pre-gebelin.blog spot.com/2013/07/.

66. "Hanged Man and Death . . . The Tarot Trumps, Some History, from Christian Beginnings to the Esotericists and C.G. Jung," tarotchristianbasis, http://tarotchristianbasis. blogspot.com/2016/11/hanged-man-and-death.html.

67. Till-Holger Borchert, Joshua P. Waterman, eds., *The Book of Miracles* (Taschen, 2014). Note- This is a faithful reproduction of a 16th century illustrated manuscript.

68. "How did Judas Iscariot Die? Why two biblical stories can't both be right, and why it matters," christiantoday. com, https://www.christiantoday.com/article/how-did-judas-iscariot-die-why-two-biblical-stories-cant-both-be-right-and-why-it-matters/62852.htm. Note- In short, the Bible has Judas hanging himself from a tree but also falling head first down onto a field where he burst open. So, he is right side up in one story, strung up and upside-down in the other.

69. Irven M. Resnick, *Marks of Distinctions: Christian Perceptions of Jews in the High Middle Ages* (Washington: The Catholic University of America Press, 2012), 151.

70. Sir James Frazer Wordsworth, *The Golden Bough* (Hertfordshire: Reference, 1993).

71. This is a difficult claim to tie to a specific citation because writings on this point are usually compartmentalized

(death in Victorian literature, death in 19th century American art, etc.). The shift can be seen in various ways, music is one that has always stood out to me. Traditional American music, such as in the seminal Harry Smith *Anthology of American Folk Music* for instance, usually have death as a common and notable feature. This is in stark contrast to popular music today.

72. "13 Unlucky for Iranians Too," realclear.com, http://www.realclear.com/offbeat/2014/04/03/iranians_avoid_bad_luck_with_outdoor_festival_6408.html

73. Todd A. Salzman, Michael G. Lawler, *Virtue and Theological Ethics: Toward a Renewed Ethical Method* (Maryknoll: Orbis Books, 2018).

74. "Tompkins Square Park," nycgovparks.org, https://www.nycgovparks.org/parks/tompkins-square-park/monuments/1558.

75. Plato, *Charmides* (350 BCE).

76. Joseph Campbell, *The Power of Myth* (New York: Anchor Books, 1988), 190.

77. "Orthodox Church Quotes," orthodoxchurchquotes.com, http://www.orthodoxchurchquotes.com/2013/11/06/st-ephrem-of-syria-virtues-are-formed-by-prayer/.

78. Willie Drye, "Atlantis," National Geographic nationalgeographic.com, https://www.nationalgeographic.com/archaeology-and-history/archaeology/atlantis/.

79. Adam Darlage, "Lightning Strikes and Divine Disfavor," The University of Chicago, Divinity School, https://divinity.uchicago.edu/sightings/lightning-strikes-and-divine-disfavor-adam-darlage.

80. Ian Brown, "Churches With Detached Towers," Google Sightseeing, http://www.googlesightseeing.com/2012/10/churches-with-detached-towers/.

81. "Lightning Strikes in Medieval Florence," medievalists.net, http://www.medievalists.net/2015/03/lightning-strikes-in-medieval-florence/.

82. Fred Gettings, *Tarot: How To Read the Future* (Stamford: Longmeadow Press, 1993), 86-87.

83. Sister M. Danielle Peters, "Flight Into Egypt," udayton.edu, https://udayton.edu/imri/mary/f/flight-into-egypt.php.

84. Rualdo Menegat, "The discovery of the modern Earth by René Descartes: The difficult scientific revolution of the terrestrial spheres," researchgate.net, https://www.researchgate.net/publication/290946976_The_discovery_of_the_modern_Earth_by_Rene_Descartes_The_diffi cult_scientific_revolution_of_the_terrestrial_spheres.

85. Frances Farabaugh, "By the Light of the Moon: Invertebrate Lunar Calendars," Smithsonian Museum of National History, https://nmnh.typepad.com/no_bones/2015/02/by-the-light-of-the-moon-invertebrates-lunar-calendars.html.

86. Editor Kathleen Martin, ed., *The Book of Symbols: Reflections on Archetypal Images* (Cologne: Taschen, 2010), 296-298.

87. Euripedes, *Helen* (412 BCE).

88. George Lundskow, *The Sociology of Religion: A Substantive and Transdisciplinary Approach* (Los Angeles: Grand Valley State University Pine Forge Press, 2008), 70.

89. The Bible, Revelation 21:5.

90. The Bible, Revelation 20:1.

91. The Bible, Revelation 8:7.

92. Andreas Andreopoulos, *Metamorphosis: The Transfiguration in Byzantine Theology and Iconography* (Crestwood: St. Valdimir's Seminary Press, 2005), 240.

93. Dev Archer, "Creation Center Sacred Symbolism of Vesica Piscis," creationcenter.org, https://creationcenter.org/sacred-symbolism-vesica-piscis/.

94. The Rubin Museum, https://rubinmuseum.org/collection/artwork/akshobhyavajra.

95. "The Enduring Allure of Tarot," catholic.com,_https://www.catholic.com/magazine/online-edition/the-enduring-allure-of-tarot.

96. The Bible, Revelation 4:7.

97. Jacob Burckhardt, *The Civilization of the Renaissance Italy* (London: George Allen and Company, 1914), 427.

98. X Maximilian J. Rudwin, "The Origin of the German Carnival Comedy," Journal of English and Germanic Philology, Vol 18, No. 3, July 1919, pp. 402-54.

99. Sir James Frazer Wordsworth, *The Golden Bough* (Hertfordshire: Reference, 1993), 301-307.

100. Gertrude Moakley, *The Tarot Cards Painted by Bonifacio Bembo for the Visconti-Sforza Family: An Historical and Iconographic Study* (The New York Public Library, 1966).

101. Eliot Weinberger, "China File What Is the I Ching?," www.chinafile.com,___http://www.chinafile.com/library/nyrb-china-archive/what-i-ching.

102. trionfi.com IN SEARCH OF TAROT SOURCES - AFTER 15 YEARS by Franco Pratesi, 11.07.2012_http://trionfi.com/search-tarot-sources.

103. Barbara Walker, *The Secrets of the Tarot: Origins, History and Symbolism* (U.S. Games Systems, Inc., 2019)

104. Carl Jung, *Memories, Dreams, Reflections* (New York: Vintage Books, 1961), 159.

105. "Jung – Sea of Faith BBC Documentary Part 1 of 2," YouTube.com, https://urldefense.proofpoint.com/v2/url?u= https-3A__youtu.be_RWB8Gx2j0R0&d=DwICAg&c=y-0b5JdTFhB3u8tci0df_jw&r=zMZOZ83X-dvY44UDN-41fEA&m=-0YEMISe7YyeBhuSntcP5kKsxlMQ6SQM3u_ yv1v391Q&s=Ck7pl7ObxOAQDWhbc_wzQ0Oq9g2Q_ kYj7nQ9IU3UCq4&e.

106. Ibid.

107. Ibid.

108. Ibid.

109. Eduardo Sturzeneker Trés and Sonia Maria Dozzi, Brucki, "Visuospatial Processing: A Review from Basic to Current Concepts," ncbi.nlm.nih.gov U.S. National Library of Medicine National Institutes of Health- National Center for Biotechnology Information, https://www.ncbi.nlm. nih.gov/pmc/articles/PMC5619126/.

110. Ravi K. Puri Ph.D., *Consciousness: The Ultimate Reality* (Bloomington: Author House, 2017).

111. Alejandro Jodorowsky and Marianne Costa, *The Way of Tarot: The Spiritual Teacher in the Cards* (Rochester: Destiny Books, 2009), 23-24.

112. Barbara Walker, *The Secrets of the Tarot: Origins, History and Symbolism* (U.S. Games Systems, Inc., 2019).

113. Fred Gettings, *Tarot: How To Read the Future* (Stamford: Longmeadow Press, 1993), 238.

114. Ronald Decker, Thierry Depaulis & Michael Dummett, *A Wicked Pack of Cards: The Origins of the Occult Tarot* (New York: St. Martin's Press, 1996).

115. The Bible, Exodus 25:8.

116. The Bible, John 2:19.

117. "Excerpts from 'Tradition and the Individual Talent'," tseliot.com, http://tseliot.com/prose/tradition-and-the-individual-talent T.S. Elliot.

118. Aleister Crowley, *The Book of Thoth - Egyptian Tarot* (GNU General Public License, 2018).

119. Hunter Oatman-Stanford, "Tarot Mythology: The Surprising Origins of the World's Most Misunderstood Cards," collectorsweekly.com, https://www.collectorsweekly.com/articles/the-surprising-origins-of-tarot-most-misunderstood-cards/.

120. Jungianthology podcast, "Facing the Gods: Archetypal Patterns of Existence," John Van Eenwyk, Ph.D. in religion and psychology.

121. Jungianthology podcast, "Facing the Gods: Archetypal Patterns of Existence," John Van Eenwyk, Ph.D. in religion and psychology.

122. Attributed to Hermes Trismegistus, mythical father of Hermetic philosophy.

123. "Origins of Cartomancy (Playing Card Divination)," Mary K. Greer's Tarot Blog, https://www.google.com/amp/s/marykgreer.com/2008/04/01/origins-of-divination-with-playing-cards/amp/.

124. Josh Jones, "Carl Jung: Tarot Cards Provide Doorways to the Unconscious, and Maybe a Way to Predict the

Future," openculture.com, http://www.openculture. com/2017/08/carl-jung-tarot-cards-provide-doorways-to-the-unconscious-and-even-a-way-to-predict-the-future.html.

125. "Jung – Sea of Faith BBC Documentary Part 1 of 2," YouTube. com, https://urldefense.proofpoint.com/v2/url?u=https-3A__youtu.be_RWB8Gx2j0R0&d=DwICAg&c=y0b5 JdTFhB3u8tci0df_jw&r=zMZOZ83X-dvY44UDN 41fEA&m=-0YEMISe7YyeBhuSntcP5kKsxlMQ6SQM3u_ yv1v391Q&s=Ck7pl7ObxOAQDWhbc_wzQ0Oq9g2Q_ kYj7nQ9IU3UCq4&e.

126. Kase I. Nonaka, César González Cantón, *Phronesis and Quiddity in Management: A School of Knowledge Approach* (New York: Palgrave Macmillan, 2014), 319.

127. "How Sigmund Freud's Massive Art Collection Influenced His Theories," Artsy.net, https://www.artsy.net/article/ artsy-editorial-sigmund-freuds-massive-art-collection-influenced-theories.

128. Joseph Campbell, *The Power of Myth* (New York: Anchor Books, 1988), 5.

129. Ibid.

130. Philippe St Genoux, *Tarot: How To Re-create Yourself with a Deck of Cards and Other Meditations* (Black Dog Books, 2015).

131. A.E. Waite, *The Pictorial Key to the Tarot* (New York: Cosimo Classics, 2007), 2.

132. Slate Culture Gabfest podcast, Writer and critic Stephen Metcalf.

133. T.G.H. James, *Howard Carter: The Path to Tutankhamen* (New York: Tauris Parks Paperbacks, 2006), 257.